dream
solutions
using your dreams
to change your life

HENRY REED PH.D.

dream
solutions

using your dreams
to change your life

NEW WORLD LIBRARY
san rafael
california

© 1991 Henry Reed, Ph.D.

Published by New World Library
58 Paul Drive
San Rafael, CA 94903

Cover design: Kathy Warinner
Text design: Kathy Warinner
Typography: Typecraft

ISBN: 0-931432-80-4
First Printing, September 1991
Printed in the U.S.A. on acid-free paper
10 9 8 7 6 5 4 3 2 1

This book is dedicated to dreams.
After you've used the book, you'll know why.

Acknowledgments

This book stands on the shoulders of pioneers like Carl Jung and Edgar Cayce, who reminded us of the power of dreams. Ira Progoff demonstrated just how much enlightenment can come from writing in a personal journal. The many dreamers who used this book in earlier formats and wrote me about the marvelous discoveries they made, the solutions their dreams provided, and the enhancement in self-esteem they gained from realizing what a creative resource they had within themselves, I thank for motivating me to persevere to get the book to this point in its evolution. I also thank Mark Thurston, John Van Auken, and Veronica Reed for their key roles in its creation, as well as Sandra Martin and Leslie Keenan for seeing to its delivery to a wider audience in this, its first public appearance.

Dream Solutions

dream
solutions
using your dreams
to change your life

① The Dream Quest

This is a very unusual book on dreams. There is little to read in it, but much to do with it. The most important part of the book is the part you write yourself. It is an experiment in learning by doing.

When you finish, here is what you will have accomplished:

1. You will have learned several techniques for interpreting dreams.

2. You will have learned how to use your dreams to get creative guidance on questions and problems that concern you.

3. You will have learned how to use the journal meditation technique of inspirational writing to channel the wisdom of your Higher Self.

4. You will have made meaningful progress toward answering a specific question or solving an actual problem with the guidance you perceived in your dreams and in your meditations.

The method is this: You will be asked to focus on a problem or question that you would like resolved or answered. Then, over a period of twenty-eight days you will use your dreams to develop and test a solution to your problem. Along the way you will learn techniques to help interpret your dreams and work on your problem.

By using these techniques in a real-life situation, you will overcome a frequent obstacle to learning to interpret your dreams and to receiving guidance from them—the "armchair speculation" trap—when a person sits back and speculates about the dream, but ventures no further than entertaining an interpretation that feels right. The best interpretation of a dream, and the one that will help you to further your understanding of dream interpretation generally, is the interpretation that you *apply*. By testing your interpretations, by putting them into practice, you receive feedback on your interpretation and are guided into a more refined understanding.

This method, which I call the Dream Quest, was developed on the basis of the work of Edgar Cayce and Carl Jung (two people who ventured the most toward developing a theory of dreaming as a guiding influence), together with my own research and experience. It was originally developed for the Association for Research and Enlightenment (A.R.E.), to test the general notion that people are capable of interpreting their own dreams and the more specific assertion (made by Cayce) that the application of an idea from a dream leads to dreams providing still greater insights.

Two assumptions were made in the development of this method. One is that whatever the question or problem you choose to work on, it will reflect something about you and how you are responding to your life situation. Dreams are also assumed to reflect something about you and how you are relating to your life. Dreams can then be applied to a problem area of your choice by discovering the personal issues that give rise to that choice of question or problem. The Dream Quest requires, therefore, that you be willing to engage in some introspection as you work on solving your question.

The second assumption is that dreams will speak to those issues that occupy your mind and your efforts *during the day*. Thus, you are asked to concentrate on your question during the day, to actively engage in activities during the day that are designed to help you resolve your problem.

Creative dreams in history, more often than not, came to people who were intensely focused on their work. Those dreams didn't just suddenly appear without prompting to a person who hadn't really been working on the problem. Dreams do their best, it is assumed here, when you are doing your best, in your conscious life, to work on your problem yourself.

Dream Solutions attempts to re-create a similar situation in your own life and asks you to make your daytime a "laboratory" where you try different solutions or answers with the hope that during the night, your dreams will provide you with additional clues. The assumption is that the dreams are innovative enhancers of your work efforts, not a substitute for work. So be prepared to work!

Techniques

The following are the techniques you will be using in your dream interpretations, with brief definitions.

Focus of Your Quest

The question or problem you will pose to be answered or resolved with the aid of the exercises in journal writing and dream interpretation.

Meditations in Inspirational Writing

The four weekly programmed instructions for a sequence of steps in expository writing are designed to teach dream interpretation skills as well as direct a process of creative problem-solving.

These meditations lead the dreamer through repeated cycles of preparation, incubation, inspiration, and application, the known cycle of creative discovery. You will be asked to allow your expository writing to become "inspirational" by using a special process of writing in *Dream Solutions*, a written form of meditation.

Expository writing was chosen as the medium for the Dream Quest for three reasons. First, most of us have well-developed verbal skills and know how to write. Using verbal skills is probably the easiest way to introduce people to dream interpretation. Second, writing in a dream journal is perhaps the most basic technique for learning to work with dreams. Third, self-expository writing is something you can do by yourself, alone, in the privacy of your journal. Other mediums of dream interpretation can be very helpful, but sometimes they either require you to develop a less-familiar skill than writing, or they work best when you have other people around to help you.

Self-expository writing, when focused on dreams, can be a powerful tool of self-discovery. When coupled with an involvement to solve a real-life problem or to answer a question about the "world out there," self-expository writing about your dreams can be a source of inspiration.

It does require some practice, however, to develop a mental attitude that best allows the inspiration to come through in the writing. That is, even though we are all familiar with writing, we can be prone to writer's block. To avoid this problem, you are encouraged to practice "inspirational writing," a term coined by Edgar Cayce to describe a writing form of meditation.

The easiest way to understand inspirational writing is by observing your breathing and how it operates and interacts with your awareness of it. Inspirational writing is the same as gently observing your breathing without interfering with it. In fact, before you begin each writing exercise, it helps to focus on your breathing for a moment and remind yourself that you can be aware of your breathing without stopping the flow. With inspirational writing, you are aware of the purpose of the writing, and you are aware of what you write as you write it, but you experience the writing as happening almost by itself.

To perform inspirational writing, you reverse the usual procedure of intentional writing, when you first think up what you want to say, then you record your thoughts. In inspirational writing, you begin by writing, with your purpose in mind, and you observe what you write. You are not recording on paper your thoughts, but rather you are noting in awareness what you write.

Best Guess

You will be asked to develop your current conception of the possible answer or solution to the question or problem you have posed. Over the course of the four-week venture in the Dream Quest, your Best Guess should steadily improve until it becomes a satisfactory and working solution.

Weekly Contract

Each week you will be asked to develop some form of application to test out, or put into practice, your current Best Guess solution. You'll make a contract with yourself to try your solution every day that week. By applying your Best Guess, you will be doing all you can to ensure that any dreams during the week will reflect your efforts and suggest a more creative solution.

Dream Petition

This device is a written petition to your dreams, asking for help in the search for a better answer than your current Best Guess.

Pillow Letter

The Pillow Letter serves as an aid to concentration for the incubation of a dream. At night, you put your dream petition under your pillow, literally to sleep on it!

Presleep Dream Incubation Reverie

This is a method of deep relaxation of the body after prolonged, intensive study which helps the mind let go and trust inspiration. It helps focus and prepare the mind to focus on the problem during your dreams on the study night and throughout the week.

The body is relaxed through a method that reinforces the receptivity toward inspiration. The body is tensed (raise your arm and hold it up or make fists while you hold your breath) to reflect your hard work and the attitude of effort. Then the body is released (letting go). Focusing on heaviness and warmth in the arms and legs is equivalent to dissolving the focused efforts of the day into the receptive, transformative energy of the earth's creative forces. Focusing on the breathing, the in and out of the breath, is attending to the natural flow of the creative element in air, the spirit, the source of inspiration. Letting the breath go is letting go of old thoughts. Allowing the breath to come of its own is practicing being receptive to inspiration. When that special, delicately relaxed state is achieved, where the breath seems to come and go on its own, it is possible to allow the mind to rest upon its affirmation without effort, to allow every breath that comes in to remind us of the affirmation, the message of our Pillow Letter petition to our dreams, without effort, but with every confidence of its fulfillment.

Schedule

The Dream Quest is designed on a cycle of four seven-day periods. For seven days you grapple with your question or problem, testing out your current Best Guess while you collect dreams. At the end of seven days, you work with your dreams, interpreting them to gain new insights into your efforts to solve your problem. Then the cycle repeats itself.

You will choose one night of the week as a study night, preparing to spend about three hours the same night of the week for the next four weeks, performing the Meditations in Inspirational Writing for dream interpretation. Each study night is preceded by seven mornings of dream recording. Each study night includes working with past dreams, developing an improved Best Guess, and making a Weekly Contract and writing a new Pillow Letter for the coming week. The fourth and final meditation occurs on the evening of the twenty-eighth day of dream recording. The experiment in *Dream Solutions* can thus be timed to coincide with a lunar cycle, if desired.

This schedule is one of the major design elements of the Dream Quest. Consideration was given to the timing of the cycles of work, rest, and inspiration. Because you may be inclined to modify the schedule, these considerations are presented in the rest of this chapter.

Most of us find it difficult to make room in our schedules for dreams and other nonessential activities, so the dream interpretation work was scheduled for only one night a week. That study night becomes a rather intense evening, involving about three hours of study and writing. The payoff is that such concentration of time increases the chances that you will remember a relevant dream the next morning. The rest of the week may produce no dream recall for some persons, but the intense study night should prove productive. *Research with people who have participated in the Dream Quest has indicated that the morning after a study night is the most likely morning on which an important dream will be remembered.*

The book is designed to be completed in four weeks. For four weeks, with one study night a week, you are asked to intensely concentrate on your problem or question, make what progress you can, then stop. That seems to be a realistic approach.

Some people have changed the schedule to spread out the work over a longer period of time. For example, a person might complete only the first five steps of Meditation One, then wait a few days until more dreams come, then work on a few more steps, wait a few days, and so on. In some respects, it makes more sense to pace yourself according to your inner promptings rather than adhering to the fixed, one night a week schedule. Be sensitive, however, to the possibility of diffusing your energy and losing your momentum on the problem-solving task.

If you modify the schedule to a self-paced approach but find that your dreams don't seem to be paying off for you, or if you keep changing your mind about what question or problem to work on, try following the plan designed in the book. As the example will show, you don't need an abundance of dreams to have a successful experience with *Dream Solutions.*

The Example

For each of the guided exercises, an example is given. It was specially developed to maximize the advantages of giving an example and to minimize the pitfalls of examples. Although the work represented by the example is real, it is also artificial. To create the example, a person went through the entire workbook sequence using the same dream.

Although it is highly doubtful that during your four weeks you will remember only one dream, the example demonstrates that you don't always need to have new dreams to continue the process. The example allows you to see the intent of the instruction, that is, the type of written material that may be generated. However, by always working on the same dream, the example relieves you of any tendency to compete with it in terms of the quality of the dream material or to compare your progress with the progress made in the example.

Past experience indicates that a major obstacle to achieving creative solutions in dreams is the dreamer's doubts that there is any creative material in the dream. The example shows, however, how much can be pulled out of a dream. Another obstacle is the tendency to compare oneself with others who are "creative," rather than trusting in one's own unique experience. The example encourages you to look for creative information in your dreams without suggesting what your creative dreams "are supposed to" look like.

In the appendix you will find two first-person accounts of Dream Quest experiences. They show how people can use *Dream Solutions* to make significant breakthroughs in their lives. Beware of the temptation, however, to compare yourself with others.

Getting Stuck: Going Around in Circles

A few people who have experimented with the Dream Quest have gotten stuck. Nothing seemed to work for them. The major complaint was that they seemed to repeat the same ideas over and over again. Not really getting any new ideas beyond the ones they had when they began, they felt they were going around in circles. It is possible to get stuck.

By examining in detail the written meditations recorded by these people, I discovered the nature of the problem. Here are some findings:

1. If you choose a problem that you are not really ready to work on, one that is simply too "hot" right now, it is unlikely your dreams will present you with any truly relevant material (except maybe to suggest that you back off!), and it is unlikely that you will be open enough in your writing to come up with new ideas. The first few steps in Meditation One are important in helping you choose a problem that both interests you at the conscious level and that your dreams evidence a readiness to work on.

2. If you do not develop a realistic weekly contract to apply your Best Guess solution, one that you are actually capable of carrying out in practice, either

you will become too passive to stimulate your dreams or you will become too active by attempting to perform impossible feats. Choose a middle road—not too ambitious, not too easy. Everything doesn't have to ride on the first experience with the Dream Quest. You can always do it again at a later date on a different problem or question.

3. In the writing exercises, coming up with the same ideas over and over again sometimes indicates that you are writing only what you know to be true. Such a constraint may prohibit new ideas from being formed. An attitude of playfulness and experimentation is helpful. It is OK to write material that is meaningless, irrelevant, worthless, or false. You are *not* committed to believing all that you write. In fact, it is better to suspend judgment, while you are writing, about what you write. Later in each meditation you will have the opportunity to review what you have written and to pull out the most meaningful and significant material.

What you write is less important than what you decide to do with what you have written—that is, developing applicable actions that test your new ideas is the crux of the Dream Quest.

In a previous research study conducted with two hundred people experimenting with this book, actively following through on the daily contract and taking actions to test the dream ideas was found to be the most important factor contributing to success. On mornings following days when people took action on their dream ideas, they were much more likely to remember significant dreams than they were on mornings following days when they did not put their dream ideas into actions.

If you find yourself stuck or going nowhere, check to see if you have been putting your Best Guess solution into practice each day. If you're not, that could be the problem.

Guidelines but Not Rules

The book does not produce the results—you do! *Dream Solutions* suggests experiments in writing to try and experiments in problem solving to attempt, but these suggestions don't guarantee particular results. Nor are the suggestions meant as hard-and-fast rules. Although the steps in the book have been carefully thought out and tested, they do not represent the only way to get guidance from dreams — you don't have to go by the book!

Explaining on paper how to ride a bicycle and making sure to include every detail would require a lengthy article covering many steps. It would help a beginner, but still that person would have to get on and ride the bike. To a person who already knew how to ride a bicycle, such instructions may contain some useful ideas, but would generally seem quite tedious reading. If you've never worked with your dreams before, the steps are useful in breaking down a mysterious process into steps anyone can follow. If you've worked with your dreams a lot, you may find some steps tedious because your own instincts will guide you to a more direct approach. Follow your instincts!

Approach your Dream Quest in the spirit of fun, and don't allow your seriousness of purpose to make you uptight. Don't look at this book as a monument in which you will engrave your words of wisdom for all to read from now to eternity. Rather, look at it as a playground of learning. Like a playground, it is a safe place to experiment, to play with words and ideas, to "mess around." You don't have to be neat! Relax and enjoy your adventure.

Begin Your Dream Quest

To begin, you do not need to know what problem you want to work on. The first week's exercise will help you define your focus. So please don't feel that you need to know for sure exactly what you want to focus on before you can begin the Dream Quest experience.

Begin by choosing a night of the week when you will be free to spend two to three hours working on your Meditations in Inspirational Writing for dream interpretation. On the morning of the day after your chosen study night, begin to record your dreams. (If, for example, Sunday night is going to be your study night, begin recording your dreams on a Monday morning.) Record your dreams for seven mornings and be thinking about some problem or question that you would like to have resolved. On the evening of the seventh day (that would be Sunday night if you began recording Monday morning), do

Meditation One. Meditation Two will come one week later (again on a Sunday night in this example), after seven more mornings of dream recording.

To record your dreams, keep a pad and pen by your bed. It's best if you write some notes about your dreams while lying in bed, as moving disrupts your dream recall. Some people like experimenting with dictating their dreams into a tape recorder, but don't get behind in your transcription!

It's not necessary to recall a lot of dreams in order to be successful at finding *Dream Solutions.* One dream a week would do quite well. But if you feel you need to prime the pump before starting, here's a technique that has burst many a dream dam: Every morning before getting out of bed, write down on a piece of paper whatever thoughts, feelings or images that come to mind, no matter where they may be coming from, dreams or not. Commit yourself to writing out a whole page of stream of consciousness impressions. Following that procedure will make sure that you are devoting enough time in the morning with the free flow of your thoughts to capture dream memories. Most people who follow through on their commitment to this procedure find they are recording dreams before the week is up.

Another way to help improve dream recall is to drink six to eight glasses of water each day. It's a healthy thing to do anyway, but for dreams, it insures that you'll be waking up at least once during the night. We wake up for nature's call at the end of a dream cycle, so your body will automatically be waking you up at an ideal time to recall your dreams.

The day of the week for my study night is ....

I will begin recording my dreams on a .... morning (the day after the day of my study night).

② Week One: Dream Records

Dream Record: *Day 1*

....

....

....

....

....

....

....

....

....

....

....

....

....

....

....

....

....

Dream Record: *Day 2*

....

....

....

....

....

....

....

....

....

....

....

....

....

....

....

....

....

Dream Record: *Day 3*

Dream Record: *Day 4*

....

....

....

....

....

....

....

....

....

....

....

....

....

....

....

....

Dream Record: *Day 5*

....

....

....

....

....

....

....

....

....

....

....

....

....

....

....

....

....

Dream Record: *Day 6*

....

....

....

....

....

....

....

....

....

....

....

....

....

....

....

....

....

....

Dream Record: *Day 7*

....

....

....

....

....

....

....

....

....

....

....

....

....

....

....

....

....

③ Meditation One:
Focusing the Quest

Here's What Happens

In collaboration with my dreams of the past seven days, I develop in this first meditation a specific focus for my upcoming efforts at creative problem-solving. I examine possible topics I have been thinking about and also look at what concerns are expressed in my dreams. Then I state one question or problem I would like to resolve and develop my motivation for doing so. I determine what my own Best Guess solution would be at this point in my understanding, and make a commitment to test this tentative solution during the coming week while I prepare myself to receive dreams that will critique my initial solution and suggest a more original approach.

Meditations in Inspirational Writing: *Step 1*

Read over your dreams from the past seven days. For each dream, compose (on the page to your right) two or more brief titles that best express the plot of the dream story.

Hint: Think of your dream as a movie. If it were a movie, what would be its title? Use your pen to play with the words. Inspiration will come while you're writing, not while you're thinking. Let your pen do some thinking on its own.

Example:

Dream: *I walk past my friend's house and see a cat up in a tree. I look the cat in the eye and it winks at me. I wink back and walk on.*

Titles: "Sly Cat in a Tree Look-Out"
"The Winking Cat"

Story Titles for My Dreams

Meditations in Inspirational Writing: *Step 2*

Take each dream title from Step 1 and pretend that the dream title refers to you and your life. How could that title be about you? Write a statement that explains what the title may mean in relation to you.

Hint: As you set your pencil to paper, meditate a moment on inspiration. Notice your breathing. If you relax, you can observe your breathing without interfering with it. Inspiration comes of its own, if you will allow it, or you can step in and control the coming in and the going out of the breath. As you learn to trust the inspiration in your breath, so you can trust the inspiration in your writing. Rather than thinking up something to write and then recording your thoughts, instead allow yourself to put your pen to paper and let yourself write whatever comes, observing your writing without controlling it. Set your mind to this thought: "What does this dream title say about me?" Allow your pen to be moved by your inner source of wisdom. While you focus on your dream title, let your moving pen do the thinking. Doodle with words, play around, take your time!

Example:
"Sly Cat in a Tree Look-Out"

Sometimes I sneak off to gain perspective on things. Sometimes in a situation I will climb up my thoughts to achieve a good vantage point to view a situation with sly detachment, winking to myself that I do really understand what's going on around me.

My Dream Titles Suggest Some Interesting Perspectives on My Life Situation

....

....

....

....

....

....

....

....

....

....

....

....

....

....

....

....

....

Meditations in Inspirational Writing: *Step 3*

Pick one of your dreams from the past seven days, one you like or that intrigues you. Or, choose a dream whose title suggests the most provocative thoughts about yourself. Underline five to seven key words that seem to evoke some special response.

Hint: Read the dream carefully, with the assumption that you can be sensitive to the feelings of the person who recorded that dream with those particular words. Notice that certain words create some kind of effect as you read them, an effect you can sometimes feel in your body or feel as a vague sensation. This task is not one of searching for the major symbols in the dream, but rather of seeking those words used in the dream text that may evoke personal associations.

Example:
friend… cat… tree… wink… eye… sly

I List a Few Key Words from My Dream that Evoke Some Special Feeling When I Read Them

....

....

....

....

....

....

....

....

....

....

....

....

....

....

....

....

....

Meditations in Inspirational Writing: *Step 4*

For each underlined word from your dream, make up two to three sentences about yourself using that word. Write truthful and meaningful sentences about yourself, not about the word. For example, using the word "flower," write something like, "I wish my creativity would begin to flower," not "Flowers are pretty." If the word were a person's name, try something like, "When I'm with Mary, I feel very confident about my abilities," not "Mary is my friend." Use the word to say something important about yourself.

Hint: Use your pencil to play with the word and allow the word to grow into a meaningful sentence. As you begin to make up sentences, permit yourself to be playful, to discover the play on words, to experiment. While you meditate upon the feeling of the word, let your pencil do the writing. Ignore rules of grammar and spelling. Be permissive with your pencil rather than pushy; be patient with the task at hand rather than demanding. If a word doesn't seem to yield sentences about you, try playing with rhymes and word games, jot down a few things the word reminds you of, or go on to the other underlined words and come back to this word later.

Example:

Sly: sly sly sly cat, sly shy, eye sly shy, I can be shy as well as sly… sly eye, with my sly eye upon the world from a distance I can pretend that I'm on top of things, I can forget that I'm shy. Rather sly than shy, when shy I can cast a sly eye.

Cat: cat, fat cat, fat cat, contented unto itself, the cat reminds me of sly, of being self-contained, aloof in the tree winking at me, making me wonder… I'm shy the cat is sly… I can be sly like a cat and act in a very self-contained manner, even when, especially when I'm really feeling shy. A cat on a hot tin roof, easy does it, I can tread lightly as a cat when I sense trouble or possible danger.

Friend: I'm a friend, you're a friend… I can be a friend… I would like more friends… As a friend, I can be hard to reach but when you're with me you'll like me.

Tree: Tree, me, see, up a tree… I can be up a tree in my thoughts, afraid, or not knowing how to come down. The tree of my life branches out in too few directions.

Wink: In a wink, in a blink. I never wink but I blink. I can wink at some of my faults, I can blink at my mistakes.

Eye: The eye of the beholder. I am the eye of my beholding, the mirror of my self-awareness is the eye of my I-ness. Look into my eye and you make me aware of my "I."

Using Words from My Dream, I Make Up Sentences about Myself and My Life

Meditations in Inspirational Writing: *Step 5*

Review the statements you wrote about yourself from your dream titles (Step 2) and from the words in your selected dream (Step 4). As you read these statements, ask yourself, "What things seem to be on my mind?" Jot down a few notes about the themes and concerns that come to mind as you read what you have written.

Example:
Having friends, being lonely, being shy and self-conscious. Being aloof.

I Note How My Current Concerns Are Reflected in My Dream-Title Statements and in My Dream-Word Sentences

....

....

....

....

....

....

....

....

....

....

....

....

....

....

....

....

Meditations in Inspirational Writing: *Step 6*

Set aside for the moment the thoughts you just wrote about and go back in your mind to the time when you began the Dream Quest. What questions or problems did you consider working on? Write some of the concerns, questions, or problems you've thought about trying to resolve.

Example:

When I started this project, what I was primarily concerned about was my business—how to develop more customers. I seem to have trouble getting new customers, although I do well with the ones I have. My customers do give me leads to new ones, but I don't feel I do as well as I could when meeting them.

Topics I Had Previously Considered for Clarification Through the Dream Quest

Meditations in Inspirational Writing: *Step 7*

Study what you have written in both steps 5 and 6 and make some notes about what these two sets of concerns have in common. How could you combine them into one question or area of focus? Write a tentative statement of a problem, question, or area of concern that you might consider for the Focus of Your Quest.

Example:
My concern over shyness was what was coming out through the dreamwork. My concern over getting new customers was what I had been thinking about. Does my shyness relate to my difficulty in getting new customers?

Tentative statement of focus: How might I overcome my shyness about getting new customers? Can I have better luck attracting new customers by overcoming my shyness?

Dream Interpretation Themes and Topics from My Conscious Mind Mingle as I Make a Tentative Statement about the Focus of My Quest

....

....

....

....

....

....

....

....

....

....

....

....

....

....

....

....

....

....

....

Meditations in Inspirational Writings: *Step 8*

Let's make sure you've expressed exactly the concern or problem you want to work on. To help clarify further what it is you are searching for, write an imaginary dialogue (a conversation) between

The you who has a problem or a question, *and*

The you who has answers to your questions and solutions to your problems.

Hint: As you "talk" back and forth, you may find that you already have a satisfactory answer to your question. If so, continue in the dialogue to develop a more difficult or a follow-up question. Or, you may find that by offering various answers or solutions that may be only partially satisfactory, you will become more specific in the formulation of exactly what it is you are searching for.

Example:

Q: How can I overcome my shyness?

A: Aren't you sly.

Q: Can I overcome my shyness instead of hiding it behind being sly?

A: Maybe you can be sly about overcoming your shyness.

Q: How can I do that?

A: You are shy because you are focusing on yourself through the eyes of the other person. Focus instead simply on the other person. Aren't you curious?

Q: Curious about what?

A: What is the other person like? What does the other person like, need? What is the other person interested in? How do you find out whether or not a potential customer has any need for your products and services?

Q: I worry about that a lot. I worry that the person won't find my products attractive.

A: There you go again, viewing yourself through the other person's eyes. Instead, focus on the other person and develop a curiosity about that person

36

and that person's needs and interests. That will help you determine how your products may be of service to this person's life. It's also an approach to overcoming shyness.

Q: It's true then, my concern over shyness does relate to my concern over attracting new customers.

A: I would rather you say, "finding new ways of serving people with my products" instead of being "attractive." The word "attractive" puts the focus on you again, instead of on them, and activates your shyness.

Q: How can I overcome my shyness and see new ways of serving people with my products?

A: That's a good question.

A Question-and-Answer Dialogue Between the Me Who Quests and the Me Who Knows the Answers

....

....

....

....

....

....

....

....

....

....

....

....

....

....

....

....

....

....

A Question-and-Answer Dialogue Between the Me Who Quests and the Me Who Knows the Answers

....

....

....

....

....

....

....

....

....

....

....

....

....

....

....

....

....

....

....

Meditations in Inspirational Writing: *Step 9*

Write your question or problem in the form you now want to have as the Focus of your Quest. What are you searching for?

Example:
How can I overcome my shyness and attract new customers?

A More Precise Statement of My Question or Problem: The Focus of My Quest

....

....

....

....

....

....

....

....

....

....

....

....

....

....

....

....

....

....

Best Guess: *Step 1*

You have posed a question or a problem for which you do not have an immediate answer or solution. Now determine what would be your Best Guess answer or solution. If you had nothing more than your current knowledge or understanding, what would be the best you could do to answer your question? Continue your dialogue with the answering part of yourself to find out your Best Guess.

Hint: Your Best Guess will be used in the coming week to give you a focus for your conscious efforts at problem-solving and to stimulate your dreams to provide you with a more creative solution. So, in this dialogue, allow yourself to develop what you sincerely feel is the best possible answer at this time.

Example:

Q: How can I overcome my shyness and develop new ways of serving people with my products?

A: Be curious about the other person rather than worrying about what that person is thinking about you.

Q: How will that help me get new customers?

A: I already said, you need to learn about the other person so you can make an informed presentation of your products, one that will speak to that person's needs.

Q: How would I do that?

A: Develop curiosity and ask questions. People are flattered that you take an interest in them. Rather than thinking about what you might say, think about them and what interests you in them and ask them questions of interest.

Q: I do sense that I would feel less shy if I think of them rather than me, so that is what I'll try. I would say that my Best Guess, then, would be something like this: When I meet someone, I will focus on them and find some question about them to ask so that I might better appreciate what that person is about.

A: That's a good start. See if that doesn't help you to be less shy. It may also give you some ideas about how it would help you learn more about potential customers.

In Dialogue with the Part of Me that Has Answers, I Develop My Initial Best Guess Solution to My Problem

Best Guess: *Step 2*

Why do you want to develop an answer to your question or solution to your problem? What do you have to gain? Does your problem or question pertain to negative circumstances you would like to eliminate? Will a solution to your problem or answer to your question bring about positive effects? Write as many reasons as you can think of concerning your motivations and purposes in achieving your quest.

Example:

My feelings of shyness are uncomfortable. I would like to feel comfortable. I feel lonely sometimes, even when people are around me. I would like to be able to feel close to people. I need new customers for my business if I am to survive. Finding new customers requires that I make contact with strangers. My shyness can get in the way. Feeling comfortable with strangers would help me communicate better and make it easier to find out if I could meet their needs with my products. My work would be easier; I would expend less nervous energy. That would leave me with more energy for family and to spend time with friends. I would feel better about myself. Having a better self-concept would help me in my work.

Sources of Motivation to Fulfill My Quest

Weekly Contract

In what ways can you test and apply, on a daily basis, your Best Guess answer to see how much progress you can make on your own to resolve your concern? Write some things you could do, or try, every day of the coming week to see how well your Best Guess will work. Develop these ideas into a contract for yourself, where you promise yourself that you will do certain things this coming week, every day, to see how well they work or to see what happens.

Hint: Make a realistic contract, promising to do only what you believe you can realistically do every day. To give your Best Guess a fair test, it's important that you make a plan you can actually follow through on.

Example:
Every day this week, when I meet someone new, I will think of questions to ask that person to help me appreciate what that person is about. I will see if that helps me feel less shy and see if it also helps me to get ideas about how my products and services might be helpful to a person like that.

A Contract to Myself: I Pledge to Do Certain Things on a Daily Basis to Put into Practice My Best Guess Solution

....

....

....

....

....

....

....

....

....

....

....

....

....

....

....

....

....

....

....

Dream Petition

Compose a brief petition to your dreams that follows the following format:

"If I (application of Best Guess as per contract) to my (statement of question or problem) with unsatisfactory results, then please, dreams, show me a better way."

Hint: The petition to your dreams is meant to focus your efforts toward problem solving as well as focus your receptivity toward dream guidance. Make specific reference to the Focus of your Quest and to the contents of your contract to apply your Best Guess solution.

To make it easier to memorize, word your petition as briefly as possible. Polish it until you have a clear and vivid statement, something you can easily repeat to yourself as you fall asleep each night. Spend some time creating your well-worded suggestion for dreaming.

Example:
If I manage to ask questions of each new person I meet this week, but I still feel shy and I still feel difficulty in developing new customers, then dreams, please show me a better way.

Shorter:
I'll ask questions of people I meet. If I'm still feeling shy developing new customers, dreams show me a better way.

I Write a Petition to My Dreams: Provide Me with Better Guidance if My Own Best Guess Doesn't Work Out

Pillow Letter

Copy the petition onto a separate piece of paper. Tonight, put it under your pillow. It becomes a Pillow Letter for you to sleep on every night this week. During the day, carry the Pillow Letter with you to remind you of your contract.

Every night this week (beginning tomorrow night, Night 8), before you go to bed, write in your journal about your efforts to fulfill your daily contract. What did you do and what happened? Then put your Pillow Letter under your pillow to sleep on it!

For the next seven mornings, record your dreams. One week from today, same time, same place, same day of the week, you will go over the dreams you have collected, interpret them using Meditations in Inspirational Writing, and look for clues that troubleshoot the problems with your Best Guess solution. Your dreams will give you clues to a better way!

Good dreams!

Presleep Dream Incubation Reverie

Our dreams naturally tend to weave themselves around what is on our minds as we fall asleep. You may be quite tired after performing the Meditations in Inspirational Writing, and the following procedure may help you relax and unwind while allowing your mind to passively focus its receptivity toward a helpful dream.

The first part of the procedure is to aid relaxation:

While lying in bed, hold your arm up slightly from the bed. Experience the effort required to resist the pull of gravity. Gradually yield to gravity, allowing your arm to sink slowly back to earth, back upon your bed. Experience the pleasure of letting go, of giving in to gravity, of letting the bed support you. You have done all you can to work on your problem, and you are now entitled to relax. You relax as you allow yourself to experience your arms and legs as heavy. Experience the pleasure of the sensation of heaviness as you let go of your problem and let the bed support you. As you focus on the experience of warmth in your arms and legs you feel at peace. Focus gently, gently on your breathing, following it in and out. As you exhale, let the breath go, and release yourself from the control of your breathing. Give in to expiration with a peaceful sigh of relief, and then allow your next breath to come to you on its own. Trust in your breath, and as you inhale, think, "it breathes me"... let go of your breath and trust in inspiration ... as the breathing goes out, let your arms and legs let go in relaxation; as the breathing comes in, trust in inspiration, and let your mind float on the words of your dream petition ... as the breathing goes out, relax; as the breathing comes in, trust in the inspiration from your dreams.

④ Week Two: Dream Records

Dream Record: *Day 8*

Contract Fulfillment Report: *Night 8*

....

....

....

....

....

....

....

....

....

....

....

....

....

....

....

....

....

....

Dream Record: *Day 9*

....

....

....

....

....

....

....

....

....

....

....

....

....

....

....

....

....

Contract Fulfillment Report: *Night 9*

Dream Record: *Day 10*

....

....

....

....

....

....

....

....

....

....

....

....

....

....

....

....

....

Contract Fulfillment Report: *Night 10*

Dream Record: *Day 11*

....

....

....

....

....

....

....

....

....

....

....

....

....

....

....

....

....

....

Contract Fulfillment Report: *Night 11*

Dream Record: *Day 12*

....

....

....

....

....

....

....

....

....

....

....

....

....

....

....

....

....

Contract Fulfillment Report: *Night 12*

Dream Record: *Day 13*

....
....
....
....
....
....
....
....
....
....
....
....
....
....
....
....
....

Contract Fulfillment Report: *Night 13*

Dream Record: *Day 14*

....

....

....

....

....

....

....

....

....

....

....

....

....

....

....

....

....

⑤ Meditation Two:
Troubleshooting Mistaken Notions

Here's What Happens

I review my dreams for clues in my quest for the resolution to my problem. I use the techniques of *scenario analysis* and *personal symbol translation* to interpret one dream as a story-like reflection of the psychology of my situation. These insights enable me to view differently my problem and my efforts to fulfill my daily contract to test my Best Guess solution to my problem. To compensate for something I may have neglected or mistaken, I have an informative encounter with a troublesome *dream symbol*. From this conversation I develop an idea about how I may have been blocking the resolution to my problem. I also explore any sources of conflict about resolving my problem and examine my readiness to sacrifice any benefits of not having my problem resolved. I reformulate the statement of my problem and rethink my Best Guess solution. I write a new contract to fulfill next week and prepare a Pillow Letter petition to my dreams for further assistance.

Meditations in Inspirational Writing: *Step 1*

Review briefly your writing from the previous week's meditation. Review what went into the development of the statement of your problem, the Focus of your Quest, and your initial Best Guess solution. Review your daily notes about your efforts at fulfilling your contract to apply your Best Guess. On the next page make a few notes about how well your efforts seemed to work toward solving your problem.

Example:
Most every time I met someone, I thought about asking the person some questions. Sometimes I had trouble thinking of what questions to ask. Sometimes asking the questions made me even more self-conscious, as if I were conducting an interview.

Notes on Reviewing Last Week's Work

Meditations in Inspirational Writing: *Step 2*

Read over your dreams from the past week.

Note: If you recall no dreams, review the dreams from the previous week and use them in the exercises for the second meditation. If necessary, all four meditations can be done using the same dream: the example demonstrates this fact. However, you may also choose to postpone working on the second meditation for another week to allow yourself to have more time to remember additional dreams. Before deciding to postpone your work, however, read "Scheduling" in the introduction to this book.

As you read the report of each dream, ask yourself, "What's the story?" Try to sense the action plot of the dream—the essence of the story line. The action plot emphasizes the verbs in the dream, that is, what is happening.

An action plot is a short statement of what transpires during the course of the dream. To emphasize the structure of the action, all mention of symbols is avoided. The themes of typical action plots are someone is trying to escape from something; someone is trying to make something new from something that is old and worn out; or someone feels neglected.

To extract the action plot, it helps to perform a scenario analysis, replacing nouns with indefinite pronouns (such as "somebody," "something") and emphasize the verbs in the dream—what is happening, the action.

For example, a scenario analysis of the nursery rhyme "Mary Had a Little Lamb" might read, "Someone has something that follows them predictably alongside."

To conduct a scenario analysis of a dream ask, "What's happening? What's the story?" to obtain the essential action plot of the events in the dream. It's one way to help recognize the relevant context of the dream, that is, what aspect of your life the dream may be responding to. The action plot may reflect a similar situation in your life.

Study the following sample dreams and the suggested action plots:

Dream: *I am in a community and we are all building houses, each person his own house. I see a woman who is stealing lumber from a young man who is trying to build his own house. I know that the young man will never be able to finish if she keeps doing this.*

Action Plot: Someone is preventing another from finishing something.

Dream: *I am walking alone on the beach. The ocean is beautiful, and I feel strength and peace from it. Then I come to an area of huge boulders and ravines that block my passage. It seems too dangerous to go on. I feel frustrated. As I begin to wake up, I have the feeling that I could have flown over the obstacles, but it is too late.*

Action Plot: Not using available capacities to overcome obstacles that block progress.

Dream: *I am in the den adjusting the TV. I have a remote-control device that rotates the antenna on the roof. I get upset because I cannot find an antenna position that will result in a clear picture for all stations. One of the programs on one of the stations is "The Search for Tomorrow."*

Action Plot: Feeling frustrated at not being able to find a position that accounts for all possibilities.

Dream: *An old man—a Catholic priest—takes a young man aside and says to him, "You will be able to see the future and help people for one year. But at the end of the year, you will die." At this point the old man falters. I realize that he is passing the ability on to the young man, and as a result it is time for the old man to die.*

Action Plot: Someone is dying and someone else is taking over.

Dream: *A lady tells me that some people are trying to make a key for a truck from an old smooth one, but it doesn't work. The new one fits in the keyhole but it won't start the engine. She says that if they cannot get it to work, they can make a duplicate from the key that came with the old one, which they've never used.*

Action Plot: Someone is trying to make something new from something that is old and worn out.

Now read through your dreams of last week and try to develop a feeling for the action plot of each dream. Then, for each dream, conduct a scenario analysis, and then write the action plot. Simply state what is happening. Avoid analyzing or interpreting the meaning of the events, or drawing conclusions or inferences. Try to write only a statement of what's happening.

Example:
Dream: *I walk past my friend's house and see a cat up in a tree. I look the cat in the eye and it winks at me. I wink back and walk on.*

Action Plot: Someone walks by something in an elevated location and pauses for an exchange of something.

The Action Plots of My Dreams

Meditations in Inspirational Writing: *Step 3*

Something similar to the action plot in your dream may be happening in your life, in some area related to your problem or the concern that makes up the Focus of your Quest. The action plot may resemble a feeling you have concerning your problem or your attempts to apply your Best Guess to your problem. For each action plot, write a sentence or two about how such a plot may reflect something going on in your life.

Hint: As you set your pencil to paper, meditate briefly on your breathing. Let your pencil do the writing. Play with the words and phrases of your action plots. Let the natural flow of your writing prompt ideas about connections to your life.

Example:
Action Plot:

"Somebody walks past something in an elevated position and pauses for an exchange of something."

Personal association:

Going by something in an elevated position reminds me of shyness. Something is exchanged—reminds me of when I meet someone and we exchange conversation. If I look up to them, then I feel that they are looking down on me and I feel shy. If I am curious about them, then I feel like I am looking down on them. I have had a bit of trouble being curious about the people I meet, trying to ask them questions without seeming that I was interviewing them. I am trying to learn how to effect an exchange. I try to help the person with their needs in exchange for their being my customer.

The Action Plots of My Dreams Remind Me about Aspects of My Life Situation Related to the Focus of My Quest

....

....

....

....

....

....

....

....

....

....

....

....

....

....

....

....

....

....

Meditations in Inspirational Writing: *Step 4*

Choose one dream whose action plot seems most related to your struggles to apply your Best Guess solution to the Focus of your Quest. List the main symbols in the dream, that is, the important nouns and verbs (together with their modifiers, if you like) in the dream.

Example:
Nouns: house, my friend's house, cat, cat up in a tree, tree, eye.

Verbs: walk, walk past, see, look, wink, walk on.

The Symbols (the Nouns and Verbs) In My Chosen Dream

....

....

....

....

....

....

....

....

....

....

....

....

....

....

....

....

....

....

Meditations In Inspirational Writing: *Step 5*

For each symbol you listed, write your definition of what that symbol means to you. Try to state your definition in a brief phrase.

Example:
House: a place to live.

My friend's house: a place where someone I like lives.

Cat: self-sufficient instinct.
Cat up in a tree: self-sufficient instinct making itself comfortable, safe and observant.

Tree: natural growth.

Eye: the focus of seeing and knowing.

Walk: natural, self-propelled motion.
Walk past: natural motion in relation to environment.

See: become aware of.

Look: Concentrate for further awareness.

Wink: creating awareness of the channel of communication.
Wink back: confirming awareness of the channel of communication.

Walk on: natural motion continues.

The Personal Meanings of the Symbols in My Dream

....

....

....

....

....

....

....

....

....

....

....

....

....

....

....

....

....

....

....

Meditations in Inspirational Writing: *Step 6*

Now that you have defined your symbols, substitute your definitions for the original symbols that make up your dream story to achieve a rough translation of the dream into your own terms. As you rewrite the dream, substituting your definitions for the (modified) nouns and verbs in your dream, add the following to the definition phrases that are being substituted in:

To the end of phrases substituting in for nouns, add the ending phrase "part of myself" to suggest that the symbol reflects something about you.

To the beginning of phrases substituting in for verbs, add the beginning phrase "I have myself" to suggest that the action reflects some expression of yourself. That is, "I have myself going uphill slowly," suggests that you are expressing some feeling of effort.

Example:
(I have myself) in *self-propelled, natural motion in relation to the environment*, in relation to *a place where someone I like lives* (part of myself) and (I have myself) *become aware* of a self-sufficient instinct (part of myself) *making itself comfortable, safe and observant* in the *natural growth* (part of myself). (I have myself) *concentrate for further awareness* at the *self-sufficient instinct* (part of myself) in the *focus of awareness and knowing* (part of myself). (I have myself) the *self-sufficient instinct* (part of myself) *create awareness of the channel of communication* with me (part of myself). (I have myself) *confirm awareness of the channel of communication*. (I have myself) *continuing in natural motion*.

A Rough Translation of My Dream with My Personal Definitions Substituted for the Symbols

Meditations in Inspirational Writing: *Step 7*

Edit and modify your translation to make it read smoothly or to help it make sense. As you smooth the text of your dream translation, think about what you wrote concerning the relation between you and the action plot of the dream (in Step 3). Do any changes in the symbol definitions come to mind?

Hint: In rewriting your dream, you are changing its form from a story to something more like a psychological statement that describes something about you and your situation.

Example:
I have myself in natural, self-propelled motion in relation to my environment and to a place where a someone-who-I-like part of myself lives. I have myself become aware of a self-sufficient instinct part of myself that is making itself comfortable, safe, and observant within a position of natural growth. I have myself concentrate for further awareness of this self-sufficient instinct in the part of myself that is the focus of seeing and knowing. I have the self-sufficient instinct part of myself create awareness of a channel of communication and I confirm awareness of this channel and have myself in natural motion continuing.

Smoother still:

As I experience the world in a natural flow of movement, I become aware of someone within me who is instinctively self-sufficient, someone who feels quite comfortable, safe, and observant. I like its feeling of natural growth. As I attune to this consciousness, this way of seeing and knowing the world, I feel its awareness within me, and its accepting me, and I continue in a natural flow of movement.

A Smoother Translation of My Dream

Meditations in Inspirational Writing: *Step 8*

What does the translation of your dream suggest to you? What does it seem to be saying? Write an interpretation of your dream based on your translation.

Example:

I seem to be in contact with a part of myself that is like an instinct, something that feels self-sufficient and in the know. It seems like a channel of communication between this instinct and myself has been opened and acknowledged. The emphasis seems to be on natural growth and self-confidence. It seems very positive and encouraging.

My Interpretation of the Dream

Meditations in Inspirational Writing: *Step 9*

How does your interpretation apply to the Focus of your Quest? Write as many connections as you can think of between your interpretation of your dream and the question or problem that has been the Focus of your Quest.

Example:

My focus concerns overcoming shyness and obtaining new customers. In the dream I am meeting someone. We exchange glances and communicate through a wink. Who I meet is above me, suggesting the possibility that I might feel nervous. I do feel a bit self-conscious in the dream. The interpretation suggests that what I am meeting is my instinctive self-sufficiency and self-confidence. I know that I do feel a bit awkward thinking of myself as naturally self-assured, so if I did meet that part of myself I would feel a bit shy about it. On the other hand, meeting a part of myself that does feel self-sufficient would seem to be exactly what it was that I am questing for, so this dream symbol could be right on target.

How My Dream and My Dream Interpretation Relate to the Focus of My Quest

....

....

....

....

....

....

....

....

....

....

....

....

....

....

....

....

....

....

Meditations in Inspirational Writing: *Step 10*

Review your notes from Step 1. How does your dream and its interpretation relate to your efforts to fulfill your daily contract and apply your Best Guess solution to your problem? Write as many connections as you can think of between your dream (with its interpretation) and what you have experienced this week as you attempted to apply your Best Guess solution.

Example:
My contract was to be curious about the people I meet and to think of questions to ask them. For the most part I was able to remember to do that, although I sometimes found it difficult to think of questions. At first, the process of thinking up questions made me self-conscious and I felt more aware of my searching for questions than really being aware of the other person. Asking the questions didn't seem too natural, like a gimmick, but more; it was that I felt like I was interviewing the person. Unlike the dream, where the wink seemed to suggest some kind of mutual understanding, I didn't have that same feeling of comfortableness asking the people questions. I did realize, however, that I was on the right track, because focusing on the other person did help me to stop thinking about what they might be thinking about me.

I would like to feel as comfortable as the cat did in my dream. I guess I need to keep working on this, so that the process of asking questions as an expression of curiosity and interest becomes more instinctive. Also, the process of thinking about questions did make me become more aware of how I interact with people. This awareness makes me feel even more uncomfortable, but I can see that it will eventually help me to reach my goal by allowing me to develop new ways of relating. The message in the dream seems to be to relax and make myself comfortable. Can I make the other person comfortable? That would seem to be just as important, and maybe really more to the point.

Here's What My Dream and Its Interpretation Suggest about My Attempts to Apply My Best Guess Solution

....

....

....

....

....

....

....

....

....

....

....

....

....

....

....

....

....

Meditations in Inspirational Writing: *Step 11*

Can you think of any mistaken notions that influenced how you stated your question or problem? Can you think of any mistaken notions that influenced you into a false preconception of what an answer or solution might be? Considering the experiences you had attempting to apply your Best Guess solution and what your dream interpretation had to say about your experience, write anything that comes to mind about what you may have neglected, misunderstood, underestimated, or miscalculated in the formulation of the Focus of your Quest or in how you have been searching for a solution.

Example:

I can see that I need to pay attention to both thinking and feeling. In trying to overcome the feeling of shyness, I directed my attention away from myself to thinking about questions to ask the other person. Although I can see that the redirection of attention is important, I learned that the added awareness that my search requires also creates another source of uncomfortable feelings. To overcome shyness, certain skills may be necessary, but also, I need to work on my feelings themselves. I need to both redirect my attention and practice feeling comfortable. I also need to consider these things in relation to the other person. Can I make the other person feel comfortable?

Some Mistaken Notions I've Discovered about My Formulation of the Focus of My Quest and about My Search for a Solution

Meditations in Inspirational Writing: *Step 12*

Examine the dream just interpreted and look for an image of a person, animal, thing, or activity that is hurting, in bad shape, broken, upset, ignored, angry, in danger, ugly, scary, sick, failing, desperate, troubled, or troubling to you in some way.

Write an imaginary conversation (a dialogue) with this image. Begin with the usual introductions, then focus on what is troubling about this image. Find out how the image feels about the matter. Find out what would make the image feel better or become OK. (If you feel it is important, you may work with an image from a different dream.)

Example:
There seems to be no image in my dream that is troubled. One image does trouble me, however, and that is the phrase, "past my friend's house." I wonder which friend, and why I walked past it.

Me: Hello there, "My Friend's House."

MFH: Hello. Nice of you to greet me. You walked right past me in your dream.

Me: So you noticed. I was wondering about that myself. Did I hurt your feelings? I'm sorry.

MFH: Well, I feel better just for your having taken the time now to visit with me. I'm your friend's house—that's a nice place to visit, you know.

Me: Yes, but which friend?

MFH: I don't know if that makes so much difference. Just think, for a moment. What does it feel like when you visit at your friend's house?

Me: I feel comfortable.

MFH: Yes, and I feel good having you here.

In Dialogue with a Troubling Image I Learn What It Needs to Become OK

....

....

....

....

....

....

....

....

....

....

....

....

....

....

....

....

....

Meditations in Inspirational Writing: *Step 13*

Continue your dialogue with the troubling image, this time reversing the focus back to yourself, telling the image what it is that is troubling you. See if the image can offer you any help or advice.

Hint: Perhaps what the image needed to become OK will suggest something similar you need to help your search. Perhaps the troubles the image was having relate to the troubles you've been having in seeking a solution to your problem.

Example:

Me: I do feel comfortable here with you, My Friend's House. Let me tell you what's happening with me and maybe you can help. I'm searching for a cure for my shyness and for feeling better about getting new customers for my business. I can feel shy around new prospects and would like to learn how to relate to them in a better way. I've been practicing a new approach when I meet people—thinking of questions to ask them as a way of getting my attention off myself, and as a way of learning more about the person and how I might serve their needs were they to become a customer. This new approach does seem to help with my shyness, but I find that I feel a bit awkward asking them all those questions, and I don't feel that the interchange is really smooth and comfortable.

MFH: Comfortable. It's comfortable here, isn't it? Don't I make you feel at home?

Me: Yes, you do make me feel at home.

MFH: How do you treat the people you meet? Do you make them feel at home? Do you treat them like a friend?

Me: I hadn't thought about that. No, I probably treat them like a challenge, someone with whom I'm going to try a new method of relating.

MFH: Just as you passed me by, in your search for new customers and a way of eliminating shyness, you passed by the importance of friendship.

Me: But I'm not really looking for friends, although I wouldn't mind having more. I'm looking for customers.

MFH: Yes, but the spirit with which you approach this is very important. Your idea about asking them questions is a good one, but first, and more important, you must approach people in an attitude of friendship, offering to make them feel at home.

Me: How do I make someone feel at home, especially when I meet them at some business location?

MFH: How do I make you feel at home? I am but a space. What kind of space do I offer to you?

Me: Comfort, acceptance, a relaxing atmosphere. I don't feel on guard, or that anything is expected of me.

MFH: How might you act toward someone you've met that would create similar feelings in them, as if you were providing them a space where they could feel comfortable and relaxed?

Me: That's something for me to think about. Thank you.

In Dialogue with a Troubling Image: I Learn How a Troublesome or Mistaken Notion May Have Blocked a Solution to My Problem

....

....

....

....

....

....

....

....

....

....

....

....

....

....

....

....

....

In Dialogue with a Troubling Image: I Learn How a Troublesome or Mistaken Notion May Have Blocked a Solution to My Problem

....

....

....

....

....

....

....

....

....

....

....

....

....

....

....

....

....

....

Meditations in Inspirational Writing: *Step 14*

Can you think of any reasons why you may not want to develop an answer to your question or a solution to your problem? Do you have anything to gain by your question remaining unanswered or your problem remaining unsolved? Write as many "benefits" as you can think of that may exist for you as long as your quest remains unfulfilled. In your particular situation, how may "ignorance be bliss"?

Example:

Why would I *not* want to develop new customers? Why would I *not* want to overcome shyness? What benefits could I possibly get from having few customers, from feeling shy? Having fewer customers means less work, but also less money. Feeling shy does protect me from getting hurt or feeling rejected. If I were less shy, I would be more outgoing, and sometimes I would be rejected. Could I tolerate that? I guess not; otherwise, I wouldn't protect myself from it so much. I guess I also protect myself from failure by my shyness. I can say that if only I weren't shy, I would have more customers. I really do have a fine product and have no need to change my wares or adopt new lines of products. The only problem is my shyness. If I overcame my shyness and were outgoing with new, potential customers, trying to learn how I could best serve them, I might learn that my products were sometimes inadequate, and I would have to worry about developing new products. I can see that I protect the status quo by my shyness and by not attracting new customers.

Benefits I Receive While My Quest Remains Unfulfilled

....

....

....

....

....

....

....

....

....

....

....

....

....

....

....

....

....

Meditations in Inspirational Writing: *Step 15*

Are you willing to let go of the benefits to fulfill your quest? Review your motivations and purposes to fulfill your quest (Meditation One, Step 11). Then, for each benefit of an *un*fulfilled quest you listed in Step 14, write how your motivation to solve your problem may help you let go of such a benefit. Write how you believe you will be able to let go of the benefits of not having your quest fulfilled.

Example:

I want to feel less lonely and I want to expand my business without straining myself. These are my positive motivations. How can they help me sacrifice the benefits of not fulfilling my quest? How can the positive motivations guide me in sacrificing the status quo? I will be giving up something familiar for something strange, but I will be giving up something that is lonely and uncomfortable for something that is exciting and rewarding. Am I ready for that? Am I ready to consider the possibility of thinking of changes in my line of products? Am I ready to accept the possibility of rejection by some people when I am outgoing? I would like to think so, but I don't know for sure. It's more frightening to let go and be outgoing, with the possibility of being hurt, than it is to hold back, stay shy, yet be protected, even if it is lonely. But I can sense the quality of adventure that would come into my work and the sense of excitement that would come into my life. I must somehow take the chance!

My Motivations and Strategies for Sacrificing the Benefits of Having My Quest Remain Unfulfilled

....

....

....

....

....

....

....

....

....

....

....

....

....

....

....

....

....

Meditations in Inspirational Writing: *Step 16*

Summarize what you have learned in this meditation. In light of what you have learned, do you want to change the way you formulate the Focus of your Quest? Write the revised version of your focus.

Example:

What have I learned? I've learned the importance of feeling. For one thing, I learned that I had a feeling of security, self-confidence, and self-sufficiency inside me. I had a taste of what that felt like. I also learned that I need to project or express feeling to the people I meet. Simply acting curious and thinking up questions may not be enough, unless I can also extend a friendly feeling at the same time—that friendly feeling of being at home.

What I Have Learned So Far: A Revised Statement of the Focus of My Quest

....

....

....

....

....

....

....

....

....

....

....

....

....

....

....

....

Best Guess

Write what your revised Best Guess solution is at this point as a result of what you have learned during this meditation.

Example:

The focus remains the same—overcoming shyness about potential new customers. My Best Guess, however, has been changed, or enlarged, to include the feeling of friendship and feeling at home: feeling at home with a friend. The basic strategy remains the same—think of the other guy—both to cure shyness and to develop new customers. But the specifics have been enlarged. Besides being curious about other people and asking them questions, I want to concentrate on making them feel at home, too. I want to have that same comfortable feeling for myself. When I imagine being at my friend's house I feel comfortable, and I want to extend that same comfort to other people. In that atmosphere of comfortableness, I can ask my questions.

My Revised Best Guess Solution

....

....

....

....

....

....

....

....

....

....

....

....

....

....

....

....

....

....

Weekly Contract

Write a new contract for yourself to follow this coming week. How can you put into practice your own, revised Best Guess solution to see how far it can take you toward achieving the goal of your quest?

Hint: Doing your best with what you have at hand is the best way to induce your dreams to give you a helping hand. What can you do with your Best Guess to forge ahead toward the object of your quest? As you venture in your Dream Quest, remember that you naturally dream about what concerns you during the day, about what has been involving your efforts; therefore, if you want to dream about a more creative solution to your problem, make your problem an active, daily concern, keeping your "nose to the grindstone," and making good use of your own Best Guess. Write a contract for yourself that has you doing something specific each day to implement your Best Guess. Keep it simple.

Example:
When I meet someone, I will imagine what it feels like to be in my friend's home, feeling comfortable, and I will extend that same hospitable, accepting welcome to the person I meet, as if I were standing in for my friend. I can do this with a warm greeting and by conveying a sense of "relax, everything's OK" to the other person. Then, when I feel that person is relaxed, I can allow my natural curiosity about people to percolate questions to ask, questions that show a friendly interest. Friendliness first, relaxed curiosity second, then questions.

My Contract to Apply on a Daily Basis My Revised Best Guess During This Coming Week

....

....

....

....

....

....

....

....

....

....

....

....

....

....

....

....

....

Dream Petition

Compose a brief petition to your dreams that follows this format:

"If I (application of revised Best Guess as per contract) to my (statement of question or problem) with unsatisfactory results, then please, dreams, show me a better way."

Hint: Polish the wording of your petition to reduce it to a brief and easy-to-remember statement, something that you could easily repeat to yourself as you fall asleep each night.

Example:
If I manage to make each new person I meet feel at home, accepted within a friendly atmosphere, and to allow my natural curiosity to bring questions to mind that I might ask that person, but I still feel shy or I still feel unnatural in my interactions with the person, and don't feel that I am able to see new possibilities for helping people out through my business, then dreams, show me a better way.

Shorter and simpler:

If I make people feel at home with my friendship, and love them with curiosity, yet still feel shy of new customers, then dreams, show me a better way.

I Write a Petition to My Dreams: Provide Me with Better Guidance if My Revised Best Guess Doesn't Work Out

....

....

....

....

....

....

....

....

....

....

....

....

....

....

....

....

....

....

Pillow Letter

Copy your petition onto a separate piece of paper. Tonight, put it under your pillow. It is a Pillow Letter for you to sleep on every night this week. During the day, carry the Pillow Letter with you to remind you of your contract.

Every night this week, before you go to bed, write in your journal about your efforts to fulfill your daily contract. What did you do and what happened? Then put your Pillow Letter dream petition under your pillow to sleep on it!

For the next seven mornings, record your dreams. One week from today, same time, same place, same day of the week, go over the dreams you have collected and interpret them to look for clues to a creative and innovative improvement to your current Best Guess solution.

Good Dreams!

Presleep Dream Incubation Reverie

If you found that performing the presleep procedure suggested last week was relaxing and you wish to continue in a similar manner, here is a suggestion for this week:

First, here is a variant on the initial, relaxation procedure:

Lying in bed on your back, take a deep breath and hold it. As you do so, make fists with your hands and hold on tight. Notice the effort it takes to hold your breath and to hold on to your fists. You begin to feel tired, and you let go. Notice how good it feels to let go. Focus on your right arm and allow yourself to experience your right arm as feeling heavy. *My right arm is heavy and I let go. My left arm is heavy and I let go. My arms are heavy and I let go. My right leg is heavy and I let go. My left leg is heavy and I let go. My legs are heavy and I let go. My arms and legs are heavy and I let go.* Focus on your right arm and allow yourself to experience it as feeling warm. *My right arm is warm and I am at peace. My left arm is warm and I am at peace. My arms are warm and I am at peace. My right leg is warm and I am at peace. My left leg is warm and I am at peace. My legs are warm and I am at peace. My arms and legs are heavy and warm… I have let go and I am at peace.*

Now gently focus on your breathing, observing the in and the out of the flow of your breath. As the breathing flows out, let your arms and legs breathe out, letting go into the peaceful experience of heaviness and warmth in your limbs. As the breath flows out, let go of your breathing and let the next breath come in all by itself. Trust in inspiration. As the breath goes out, let go of your problem and trust in inspiration, letting the next breath come of its own. As the breath comes in, experience the inspiration as a prayer, an affirmation that your problem will be solved, your question answered. As the breath comes in, experience the inspiration as a prayer and visualize the troubling image in your dream having itself transformed into something positive. Allow yourself to remain in the gentle back-and-forth rhythm of your breathing, letting go as the breath goes out, experiencing the inspiration as a prayer of affirmation.

⑥ Week Three: Dream Records

Dream Record: *Day 15*

....

....

....

....

....

....

....

....

....

....

....

....

....

....

....

....

....

Contract Fulfillment Report: *Night 15*

Dream Record: *Day 16*

Contract Fulfillment Report: *Night 16*

....

....

....

....

....

....

....

....

....

....

....

....

....

....

....

....

....

....

....

Dream Record: *Day 17*

....

....

....

....

....

....

....

....

....

....

....

....

....

....

....

....

....

Contract Fulfillment Report: *Night 17*

Dream Record: *Day 18*

....

....

....

....

....

....

....

....

....

....

....

....

....

....

....

....

....

Contract Fulfillment Report: *Night 18*

Dream Record: *Day 19*

....

....

....

....

....

....

....

....

....

....

....

....

....

....

....

....

....

Contract Fulfillment Report: *Night 19*

Dream Record: *Day 20*

....

....

....

....

....

....

....

....

....

....

....

....

....

....

....

....

....

....

Contract Fulfillment Report: *Night 20*

Dream Record: *Day 21*

⑦ Meditation Three:
Searching with New Eyes

Here's What Happens

I review my experiences at fulfilling my daily contract to apply my updated, Best Guess solution. I review and title my dreams, letting the dream titles suggest new ideas about what I have learned so far. I examine a novel symbol from one of my dreams and learn from it new ideas about how to solve my problem. I recall an experience from my past when I felt at my very best and I imagine how I might use that viewpoint to suggest a different method of relating to my creativity. I contemplate the benefits to other people, or to the world at large, of my achieving a solution to my problem. From these new perspectives I view my problem from a new angle and formulate a new solution to my question that has been the Focus of my Quest. I develop a new Best Guess and contract to put it into practice this coming week.

Meditations in Inspirational Writing: *Step 1*

Review briefly your writing from last week's meditation. Review your daily efforts at fulfilling your daily contract to apply your revised Best Guess solution during this past week.

Write any new ideas you have learned about the solution to your problem from your experiences attempting to apply your revised Best Guess.

Example:
Trying to get into the feeling of friendliness has been good when I can do it, but it brings me face to face again with my shyness. But from my first week's work, I can see that the shyness has something to do with my imagining being judged by the person, there being some kind of gap or space or distance between us, and I wonder if the person will accept my gesture of friendship. On the other hand, working from a space of friendliness and curiosity, I am learning a lot about the other person and can see that it helps me to determine just how my services could best help the person. That part is definitely making me a better businessperson. I enjoy that.

Work on My Daily Contract Applying My Revised Best Guess Has Given Me These New Ideas about a Solution to My Problem

....

....

....

....

....

....

....

....

....

....

....

....

....

....

....

....

....

....

Meditations in Inspirational Writing: *Step 2*

Review your dreams from the past week. Treat each dream like a movie or a story. Make up a title for the dream story, one that suggests the plot of the story. Write the titles for your dreams of the past week.

> *Note:* If you did not recall any dreams during the past week, you may either postpone this (third) meditation for another week, thus allowing yourself seven more days to continue applying your current Best Guess while waiting for further dreams, or you may work with the dreams from the first two weeks and use them in this meditation. As the example continues to show, the entire Dream Quest and all four meditations can be used to good effect with only one dream. If you decide to postpone your work on this meditation, read the Scheduling section in the introduction.

Example:
The Cat Conspiracy

The Cat Wink Wonder

The Titles of My Dreams

....

....

....

....

....

....

....

....

....

....

....

....

....

....

....

....

....

....

Meditations in Inspirational Writing: *Step 3*

Pretend that each of your dream titles is a coded statement, giving a clue about a new possibility in the solution to your problem. For each dream title, write some ideas about what that title suggests to you about possible solutions to your problem. (If you like, you may review all your dreams to date to see what the titles of earlier dreams may suggest.)

Example:

The cat's wink makes me wonder. What is the cat trying to say? I imagine some sort of conspiracy. The cat seems to indicate that it and I are "in" on something together. How could my potential customers and I be "in" on something together? Wouldn't that help my shyness? I wouldn't wonder whether I was to be accepted, for the conspiracy suggests an established fact. How can I invite a conspiracy? Inviting the person to share my "at home" feeling seems to be on target.

The Titles to My Dreams Suggest New Ideas about Possible Solutions to My Problems

Meditations in Inspirational Writing: *Step 4*

Look through your dreams of the past week (or earlier dreams if necessary) and search for a dream that contains a novel symbol—an image of a person, thing, animal, circumstance, or activity—that in some manner seems unique, unusual, intriguing, unexpected, creative, or original.

Rewrite the dream from the perspective of this novel symbol, as if the symbol were experiencing the dream. Let the symbol tell the story of the dream as it might have experienced it.

Example:
The novel symbol in my dream is the wink of the cat. The cat itself isn't so novel, but the cat's winking is.

"Eye Wink at the Passing Stranger"

I exist within the twinkle of a cat's eye. I exist as a potentiality, awaiting the command to become visible in action, as a wink. I am the wink in this cat's eye. There is this man, walking down the street. He seems to have a wrinkled brow, lost in worry or thought as he passes by, without a glance of recognition, a house that extends him friendship. As he walks along, he approaches where I live, within this cat's eye. This cat is up in a tree, spying over all. The man stops at the tree, looks up and sees the cat. I can feel the man's eyes looking into the eyes of the cat. I am awakened, waiting, and in a twinkle, I come to be. The cat's eye winks and I AM. The man winks back, and I AM also within the man's eye. For that moment, I AM existing both within the cat and the man. The cat's eye reopens, and so does the man's, and I am but a memory. The man walks on and I dissolve back into potentiality.

My Dream, as Told from the Point of View of Its Novel Symbol

....

....

....

....

....

....

....

....

....

....

....

....

....

....

....

....

....

....

Meditations in Inspirational Writing: *Step 5*

Have a dialogue between yourself and the novel symbol. Begin by asking the symbol about itself, how it felt about the events in the dream, the role it played, and how it was treated.

Example:
Me: Hello, there, you wink in the cat's eye.

W: Howdy.

Me: How do I talk to a wink?

W: Judiciously.

Me: How's that? Must I be so careful?

W: I was just kidding. Didn't you see me? I mean, I winked.

Me: How does it feel to be a gerund—a noun that's really a verb?

W: You've got to be kidding.

Me: Well, maybe, but I'm really curious about how it feels to be you. You're not a thing, but an event!

W: Yeah, I only exist when I do my thing!

Me: How does that feel?

W: When I happen, I feel pretty good; there's generally a good feeling between me, the cat, and the person being winked at. Like with you, there was that moment of suspense when you and the cat confronted each other. Then when I came to be, when the cat winked, something happened, like the cat was communicating something to you, something contagious, because you winked back. My good friendly feeling spreads, doesn't it?

My Dialogue with the Novel Symbol Reveals Its Special Role in the Dream

....

....

....

....

....

....

....

....

....

....

....

....

....

....

....

....

....

....

....

Meditations in Inspirational Writing: *Step 6*

Continue your conversation with the novel symbol and try to learn as much as possible about the different aspects of the symbol's novelty, uniqueness, or special features.

Example:

Me: Yes, you do have some special qualities.

W: Yeah, I'm a gerund, an event, a process, a happening. It's hard to get a handle on me. If you clamp down on me, then I'm no longer a wink—instead, you just have a closed eyelid!

Me: Also, the cat's eye can't see when it's winking. To communicate the wink, the eye has to let go of seeing for a moment. To send a message, the eye has to surrender its gaze.

W: I'm full of paradox. I tease you. I make you realize that the cat has awareness. I invite you to join it; I say, "We have a little secret—let's enjoy it!"

Me: You really invite friendship, a conspiratorial comradeship. That reminds me…

My Dialogue with the Novel Symbol Reveals Its Special Qualities

....

....

....

....

....

....

....

....

....

....

....

....

....

....

....

....

....

....

Meditations in Inspirational Writing: *Step 7*

Now discuss with the novel symbol the Focus of Your Quest. Ask the symbol for its ideas about possible solutions to your problem. Brainstorm with the symbol to develop analogies between the symbol's novelty and possible new approaches to the solution to your problem. For example, if the symbol is novel because of its such-and-such quality, how might you approach your own problem in such-and-such a manner?

Example:

Me: I have this problem that I'm working on. It's about being shy when I meet people and the trouble I have developing new customers for my business when I meet new contacts. I'm wondering if you have something to offer on this problem.

W: What have you tried?

Me: What I'm working on is to think of the other guy, rather than be self-conscious, which only aggravates my shyness. I've also been trying to be curious about the other person, to ask them questions about themselves. I try to extend an attitude of friendliness, as if to make the person feel at home in my presence, at home in the space of our meeting.

W: That sounds like a really good approach. How has it worked?

Me: It works pretty well when I can do it. I can see that it has value both for overcoming my shyness and for learning about the other person to see how I might be able to serve the needs and interests through my business.

W: But you can't always do it?

Me: No, lots of times it seems contrived, and I feel just as self-conscious as always, only even more so in a way, because I'm trying to think up all these questions to ask. Trying to be friendly first helps on that score, like getting in the mood, but then trying to be friendly seems to require that I not be shy, and I seem right back where I started from.

W: Aha! That's where I come in. The paradox! When you wink, you become more lighthearted, less serious. Also, the wink blocks the eye—the self-consciousness.

Me: Tell me more!

W: Just like the eye has to let go of seeing to allow the wink to be, so also you have to let go of self-consciousness to be truly friendly and think of the other guy. You were very clever to think of that.

Me: The Me Who Knows thought of that. But I can't always do it.

W: Who is this Me Who Knows person? Isn't that the wink itself? Doesn't the wink say, "Hey, we know what's happening!" That's really funny.

Me: Yeah, you're right! Just like the wink communicates a conspiratorial friendliness, saying "Hey, we're in this together," so also does my extending friendship to the person create a bond between us, saying "Hey, we're right at home here together," so there is less a gap, a difference between that person and me, less of a need to feel self-conscious or shy. There's no me-looking-at-him-and-him-looking-at-me, instead, there's just winking! Feeling at home with a friend!

W: That's right, lose yourself in the event! The eye loses itself in the wink. The wink joins the two persons together!

Me: Yeah, two eyelids stuck together!

W: That's the spirit, keep joking. That seems to be a part of the solution, having some humor. Humor also helps to overcome the self-consciousness and to bridge the gap between you and the other guy.

Me: This has been really helpful, Wink.

W: It was nothing! Well, maybe it was a gerund that did it!

My Dialogue with the Novel Symbol Reveals Helpful Analogies Between the Symbol's Novelty and Possible New Approaches to My Problem

....

....

....

....

....

....

....

....

....

....

....

....

....

....

....

....

My Dialogue with the Novel Symbol Reveals Helpful Analogies Between the Symbol's Novelty and Possible New Approaches to My Problem

....

....

....

....

....

....

....

....

....

....

....

....

....

....

....

....

....

Meditations in Inspirational Writing: *Step 8*

Go back in your memory to a time when you felt at your very best, a peak experience when you felt most in tune with your abilities, a moment of great self-confidence, of an exalted state of consciousness. Write this experience and describe how you felt.

Example:
Dancing.

I'm dancing in the ballroom with this dear person. The music is playing one of my favorite songs and we're really flowing to the music. My dance steps and the other person's dance steps complement one another so perfectly that it's hard to tell who's leading whom or who's directing it. The dance is happening so smoothly to the music that I feel swept away. I feel as if I'm being danced around, that I'm making no effort at all to dance. It's just happening. I'm surprised that I don't have to think about the steps or count time to the music as I often do. Instead, it all works out perfectly, smoothly. I can trust myself, I don't need to worry about doing it right, and I am carried away in the dance to the flow of the music.

I Describe a Peak Experience from My Past

....

....

....

....

....

....

....

....

....

....

....

....

....

....

....

....

....

Meditations in Inspirational Writing: *Step 9*

During your peak experience, how did you feel about yourself and life? What essential truths or meanings were expressed in this experience? Compose a motto that best describes the basic truth or meaning that this peak experience holds for you.

Example:
I felt wonderful, and even though I was very active, I felt at rest, somehow, because the dance carried me along. I can see in such an experience the truth of such statements as "let go and it will all work out." Like life can take care of itself if you'll just get out of the way. It's a very different feeling than how I feel when I am shy and self-conscious.

The motto for me would be, "Trust in the Flow of the Dance."

My Peak Experience Suggests a Personal Motto: One of My Life's Greatest Truths

....

....

....

....

....

....

....

....

....

....

....

....

....

....

....

....

....

....

Meditations in Inspirational Writing: *Step 10*

Review your dream containing the novel symbol, this time from the point of view of you, the dreamer, and ask yourself these questions:

1. What am I assuming in the dream?

2. What choices am I making in the dream that may have affected how the dream unfolded?

Example:
I am assuming that there is nothing for me in my friend's house, that I don't have time to stop. With the cat, I am assuming that the cat is perched up there for a reason and doesn't want to be disturbed, that I must walk on. I choose to walk past my friend's house without stopping, I choose to wink back at the cat, I choose to walk away from the cat without further interaction.

I Examine My Assumptions and Choices in My Dream of the Novel Symbol

....

....

....

....

....

....

....

....

....

....

....

....

....

....

....

....

....

Meditations in Inspirational Writing: *Step 11*

Recalling your peak experience and the personal motto that describes what you learned from that experience, consider how you might have acted differently in your dream. If while in the dream you were following the wisdom of your personal motto, what different assumptions and choices might you have made? What different actions might you have taken? Rewrite your dream, using your personal motto to guide you in developing a new version of your dream.

Example:

I am walking down the street. I see my friend's house and stop in for a visit. We have a nice talk and I leave feeling content and happy. It's good to have friends. As I walk along, I see a cat up in a tree. I look at the cat and it winks at me. I wink back. I extend my arms and the cat jumps down out of the tree into my arms. I cuddle and pet the cat and it purrs. The cat's purr is contagious and I feel like purring myself. I feel very much at home with myself and in the world. What a wonderful place to be. I feel like welcoming others into this wonderful home we have here.

My Personal Motto Helps Me Create a New Version of My Dream

....

....

....

....

....

....

....

....

....

....

....

....

....

....

....

....

....

Meditations in Inspirational Writing: *Step 12*

Create a title for your revised dream. Analyze the scenario of the revised dream (see Meditation Two, Step 2): Write the action plot—a scenario of what happens in the dream.

Example:

Titles: "Trust in the Flow of the Dance"
"The Winking Cat and I Purr"
"Trust in the Wink of the Cat for a Purrfect Sense of Home"
"For Purrfect Trust in our Friendly Home, Cuddle the Winking Cat"

Scenario Analysis:

The Action Plot: Someone visits someone for a friendly feeling, then meets someone in an elevated position for an exchange of communication that leads to an equalizing posture and to a sharing of trust and contentment.

The Title and Action Plot of My Revised Dream

Meditations in Inspirational Writing: *Step 13*

Compare your revised dream with the original. How do the two dreams differ? Write a list of differences between your revised dream and the original version. For each difference, use the title and the action plot of your revised dream, and write what the revised version of your dream suggests to you about a different approach to the resolution of your problem.

Example:
Visiting with my friend:

Taking time for fellowship creates a better atmosphere. This feeling lasts and affects the subsequent action. I realize that in my efforts to use my Best Guess, I had not allowed for the extra time it takes. I learn here, "slow down, take your time."

Extending arms to cat:

Although I have found the extension of that at home feeling to be a useful tool in my work on this project, I realize that perhaps even some body contact, at least shaking hands if not also an arm on the shoulder, almost guiding the person physically as I offer a moment of "time out for friendship," will help overcome my problem.

My Revised Dream Suggests New Ideas about a Solution to My Problem

....

....

....

....

....

....

....

....

....

....

....

....

....

....

....

....

....

....

....

Meditations in Inspirational Writing: *Step 14*

You have contemplated three new sources of inspiration: the novel symbol, a personal motto based on a peak experience, and a creative revision of your dream. What connections can you find among the ideas generated by these three sources? Write what you have learned from these sources and how the ideas seem to relate to one another.

Example:

Novel symbol:
Letting go. Being in action—a wink—pushes aside self-consciousness. Humor. The twinkle in the eye.

Personal motto:
Trust in the flow of the dance. Becoming one with the other guy. Surrendering to the exchange of energy. Friendship as a dance.

Dream revision:
Extending an arm in friendship. Taking time out.

All these ideas do relate to one another. My ideas from the last meditation work pretty well, but sometimes my mood or habitual self-consciousness make the approach I want to take not be natural. Here I learn more about the spirit of the approach I want and two physical aids: winking!—I may even try that!—and also extending an arm. We all get so caught up in our routines, me and the other guy. If I extend an arm in friendship with a conspiratorial wink, suggesting that we take "time out!" to realize how wonderful it is simply to be alive and to enjoy the moment, I can see this helping. It takes me way beyond the shyness feeling. From what I have noticed already—about taking an interest in the other guy does make it easier to learn how I might serve that person with my business—I can see how this added dimension will help even more. In fact, I can see now that I want to add a new dimension to my business itself, that is, the way I conduct business, that the customer gets a bonus—a moment to relax and a sense of fellowship. I think that this in itself is an exciting discovery, a feeling that we are in this together!

An Integration of Ideas from the Novel Symbol, My Personal Motto, and a Creative Revision of My Dream

....

....

....

....

....

....

....

....

....

....

....

....

....

....

....

....

....

....

Best Guess: *Step 1*

In Steps 1-3, you reviewed your efforts from the past week to apply your updated, Best Guess solution, and looked to your dreams for comments upon your experience. Review now what you wrote in those three steps.

When you view your efforts from the past week in light of the insights you have gained in this meditation (summarized in Step 14), what thoughts come to you about how to change your approach to a solution to your problem? Write ideas about how you might go about things differently.

Example:
The main thing I felt still lacking was the feeling of naturalness about my solution. I could see that the ideas of curiosity, friendliness, at-home feelings, and so on was right on target, both for shyness and developing new customers. But I found still that I would stumble sometimes, and it didn't seem natural. In this third meditation, I've gotten some good ideas that are right on target. The dream image of the wink, now that I have worked with it, seems perfect for me as a symbol of what I need to remember. The memory of the dance, the good feelings and good humor—all these ideas seem to have taken my problem to a new level for resolution. I'm moving beyond the issue of shyness to considering the quality, or spirit, with which I want to confront life. Shyness about people was a concern that touched on a shyness about life. Separation, me against the elements, life, other people—that was the premise I was operating on. That made customers a challenge. The image of the wink, with that paradoxical quality of giving up seeing to express something else, that really hit me, for it led to the notion also of doing away with being on guard. The dance theme also expresses that same theme of trust. What I really like is the idea of adding a new dimension to my business, the matter of how I conduct the business. That gives me a new sense of enthusiasm for my work!

A Review of My Meditation Suggests a Different Approach to the Solution of My Problem

....

....

....

....

....

....

....

....

....

....

....

....

....

....

....

....

....

....

Best Guess: *Step 2*

Write a new version of your Best Guess solution that incorporates what you have learned during this meditation.

Example:
My earlier, revised Best Guess solution:

Extend feeling of comfortableness, at-homeness to other guy, then express curiosity.

New version:

Take your time, extend yourself *physically* in a wink or a pat on the shoulder. Establish first the "time out to feel at home" atmosphere. The other guy is just like you. Trust in the flow. Remember that your business is how you do business. Your business expresses your feelings about life.

A New Version of My Best Guess Solution

Weekly Contract: *Step 1*

How can you apply and test out your new Best Guess solution? Write a contract specifying what you will do to apply your new Best Guess on a daily basis this coming week.

Example:
What if I practiced winking? What other body cues might I use to experience and express that same feeling? I want my feelings of shyness or uptightness to signal me to take a TIME OUT to remember to trust in the flow of the dance!

While I work on that one, what I can do is promise that every time I meet a new person I will extend myself in friendship, with a wink or a touch, to say, "Take a moment to make yourself at home, us together."

My expression of interest in the other guy need not be simple, mundane questions of curiosity, but can also be directed toward what makes that person feel good. A sense of humor reminds me that in spite of my troubles, my "soap opera," if I take a moment to realize it, life is pretty good.

I will explore the implications of this approach to business to see what develops.

My Contract to Apply on a Daily Basis My New Best Guess Solution This Coming Week

....

....

....

....

....

....

....

....

....

....

....

....

....

....

....

....

....

Weekly Contract: *Step 2*

How will other people, or the world at large, benefit from your fulfilling your quest? Write as many ways as you can think of about how your getting your problem solved or your question answered will create benefits that will extend beyond yourself.

Example:
For one thing, when I become less shy, people are going to know me better, and I think that is a good thing! I have been hiding myself from people and that cheats them. Because I have changed my view on my business relations, I can clearly see how my customers are going to benefit from my success on my quest: they are going to reap the rewards of my spending time with them on a friendly basis, they are going to have a chance to feel better about themselves, and they are going to have a chance to influence me in the products I offer, ones that will really help them. So, I am feeling really good that everyone will benefit from my fulfilling my quest!

Benefits to Others of My Fulfilling My Quest

....

....

....

....

....

....

....

....

....

....

....

....

....

....

....

....

....

Dream Petition

Compose a brief petition to your dreams that follows this format:

"If I (apply my new Best Guess solution as per contract) to my (statement of problem or question) with unsatisfactory results, then please, dreams, show me a better way."

Example:
If I take time out to extend friendly at-home trust in the flow of the dance of life, winking as I go, yet still feel shy of new customers, then dreams show me a better way!

A Petition to My Dreams: Provide Me with Better Guidance if My New Best Guess Solution Doesn't Work Out

....

....

....

....

....

....

....

....

....

....

....

....

....

....

....

....

....

....

Pillow Letter

Copy the petition onto a separate piece of paper. Tonight, put it under your pillow. This is a Pillow Letter for you to sleep on every night this week. During the day, carry the Pillow Letter with you to remind you of your contract.

Every night this week, before you go to bed, write in your journal about your efforts to fulfill your daily contract. What did you do and what happened? Then put your Pillow Letter dream petition under your pillow and sleep on it!

For the next seven mornings, record your dreams. One week from today, same time, same place, same day of the week, go over the dreams you have collected and interpret them to receive an evaluation of your progress in your Dream Quest.

Good Dreams!

Presleep Dream Incubation Reverie

In this Presleep Dream Incubation Reverie we introduce a special scene into the imagination when the quiet state of natural breathing has been established. The scene involves imagining you are in a special place, a place you would call sacred or inspired, and imagining being in the presence of a Wise Person, someone who would either be very likely to help you with the problem that is the Focus of Your Quest, or someone who would be the living example of the personal motto you developed in the third meditation.

First, establish the body's relaxation and its natural breathing. Make fists with your hands, hold your breath. Experience the effort. Let go. Step by step begin to experience heaviness in your right arm, left arm, both arms; your right leg, left leg, both legs; your arms and legs. Then, in the same step-by-step manner, experience warmth in your limbs. These steps can be finally integrated by the statement, "My arms and legs are heavy and warm. I have let go and I am at peace." Then focus on your breathing, letting go on the exhalations, letting your limbs breathe out, and awaiting the next breath to come of its own, trusting in inspiration.

Every time your breath comes in, allow your imagination to develop a scene, visualizing a special place where you would feel very comfortable, a place where you might seek inspiration, a place that would be sacred for you.

Imagine you are in your sacred place. Allow the special protective and comforting atmosphere of your place of healing to create within you a mood of serenity. Your arms and legs are heavy and warm, you have let go of your problem, yielding yourself to the support of the earth, giving in to your expirations with peaceful sighs, because you are safe within your sacred place of healing. Imagine that a revered Wise Person is approaching. Feel the special vibrations of your Wise Person's presence and experience the confidence and optimism that is inspired in you. Letting go with a peaceful sigh, trusting in inspiration … you are in the presence of your revered Wise Person, the living example of your special motto, and you are safe within your sacred place.

You have relinquished all further attempts to deal with your problem yourself. The revered Wise Person has taken over your problem for consideration and has agreed to help you. Give yourself over to anything you may now experience, and assume that whatever you do experience is part of the healing that is beginning to transpire as you fall asleep. It is a process that will continue during the night and in your dreams. When you awaken tomorrow, you can bring a new spirit to putting your Best Guess into action, knowing that the world is rooting for you to succeed and that your dreams will be guiding you to even better solutions as you do your best with what you have in hand.

Rest now, sleep now, you are safe within your sacred spot, inspiration is here, dreams are near.

❽ Week Four: Dream Records

Dream Record: *Day 22*

....

....

....

....

....

....

....

....

....

....

....

....

....

....

....

....

....

Contract Fulfillment Report: *Night 22*

Dream Record: *Day 23*

Contract Fulfillment Report: *Night 23*

Dream Record: *Day 24*

....

....

....

....

....

....

....

....

....

....

....

....

....

....

....

....

....

....

Contract Fulfillment Report: *Night 24*

Dream Record: *Day 25*

Contract Fulfillment Report: *Night 25*

Dream Record: *Day 26*

Contract Fulfillment Report: *Night 26*

Dream Record: *Day 27*

Contract Fulfillment Report: *Night 27*

Dream Record: *Day 28*

....

....

....

....

....

....

....

....

....

....

....

....

....

....

....

....

....

....

⑨ Meditation Four:
Taking Stock

Here's What Happens

I review my experiences during the past twenty-eight days of this experiment in dream solution. I examine how my understanding has developed concerning the problem I originally stated as the Focus of My Quest. I evaluate what has been accomplished and what remains to be done. I have a dialogue with a source of wisdom within myself to evaluate my work. I choose one of my dreams and practice some dream interpretation skills I have learned. I relate the understanding that I achieve from this dream to my experiment in the Dream Quest. I express this new understanding in the form of a poem written from my dream. I use this poem to guide me in my future efforts until such time that I am ready once again to embark on a Dream Quest.

Meditations in Inspirational Writing: *Step 1*

Review your efforts from this past week at fulfilling your daily contract to apply your new, Best Guess solution. What kinds of success did you have? What kinds of problems? Write some brief notes about your experiences from applying your new Best Guess solution.

Example:

I have been having a good time with my revised Best Guess. The concept of conspiracy, of us as opposed to me and them, has helped enormously. I enjoy searching for commonalities between myself and the other person. I am finding I am more relaxed with the other person because we have a sense of sharing.

My Experiences Applying My New Best Guess Solution to My Problem

....

....

....

....

....

....

....

....

....

....

....

....

....

....

....

....

....

....

Meditations in Inspirational Writing: *Step 2*

Review your written work from the past three meditations. Examine particularly the development of the formulation of your problem and your own Best Guess solution. How has the Focus of Your Quest changed over these weeks? How has your Best Guess solution changed? Write some notes about the evolution of your understanding of the problem and its possible solution.

Hint: Study in particular what you wrote in Meditation One, steps 5, 6, 7, 9, Best Guess, steps 1 and 2; Meditation Two, steps 9, 10, 11, 13, 14, 15, 16; and Meditation Three, steps 1, 3, 7, 13, 14, Best Guess, steps 1 and 2, Weekly Contract, steps 1 and 2. These are the steps in which you state the problem, make statements about your current Best Guess solution, and draw inferences from your dream interpretation work about possible solutions or develop daily contracts to apply your current Best Guess solution.

Example:

The Focus of My Quest began with an attempt to combine two different themes. I was concerned, at the conscious level, with how to attract more customers to my business. My dreams from that first week, however, seemed to be more concerned with my feelings of shyness. These were combined in my initial Best Guess—"Think of the Other Guy"—which proved to be good advice for both shyness and attracting customers. Asking questions of the other guy was my initial action to apply. I found this a useful beginning, redirecting my attention in a constructive manner, but it didn't speak to my feelings of awkwardness, and although it was designed to get me past self-consciousness, it seemed to increase it.

The feeling aspect was then dealt with in terms of friendliness and the feeling of being "at home." Interest in the other guy became making the other person feel at home. That gave me an image to concentrate on, to assume that I was hosting the other person to relax in an at-home atmosphere. That was a good image for me and did a lot to help me with my feelings of self-consciousness. Yet, I was still feeling strained; it required an effort to do. I guess I was taking it too seriously and seeing the other guy as a challenge.

The dream dialogue of the wink introduced the need for humor and for making me think less in terms of me versus the other guy and more in terms of us. Developing a personal motto, "Trust in the Flow of the Dance," gave me a larger perspective in which to view the Focus of My Quest as it now related to my general feelings about life. The conspiratorial wink had a larger purpose to it. Revising my dream helped me to see the importance of taking "time out" when I met someone, and to use physical as well as verbal communication to express the feeling of being at home with each other. I also realized that my business goal was not simply to attract more customers, but to relate to customers in a particular way so that we all could feel very good about ourselves. I have found this part of my Dream Quest to be the most exciting because it has given me a new sense of enthusiasm about my work.

Observations about the Changes in How I View the Problem and about the Development of My Best Guess Solution

....

....

....

....

....

....

....

....

....

....

....

....

....

....

....

....

....

....

Observations about the Changes in How I View the Problem and about the Development of My Best Guess Solution

....

....

....

....

....

....

....

....

....

....

....

....

....

....

....

....

....

Meditations in Inspirational Writing: *Step 3*

How would you now formulate the problem that has been the Focus of Your Quest?

Example:

Originally: Overcoming shyness, attracting new customers.

Finally: Using my business contacts as an opportunity to encourage myself and the people I meet to realize how good it is to feel at home in the world and to trust in the flow of the dance.

My Final Formulation of the Problem: the Focus of My Quest

....

....

....

....

....

....

....

....

....

....

....

....

....

....

....

....

....

....

Meditations in Inspirational Writing: *Step 4*

How would you now formulate your final, Best Guess solution to this problem?

Example:

When I meet people, taking time out to extend, both physically and verbally, a feeling of being at home with one another.

A Tentative Statement of My Final Formulation of My Best Guess Solution

....

....

....

....

....

....

....

....

....

....

....

....

....

....

....

....

....

....

Meditations in Inspirational Writing: *Step 5*

Review your dreams from this past week. For each dream, create a title that expresses the story of the dream.

Example:
"The Purrfect Wink Links Us"

Titles for the Dreams of this Week

....

....

....

....

....

....

....

....

....

....

....

....

....

....

....

....

....

Meditations in Inspirational Writing: *Step 6*

For each dream title, write some ideas that the title reminds you of concerning your efforts to apply your new, Best Guess solution to your problem. (You may perform this analysis on the titles of your earlier dreams as well.)

Example:
The purrfect wink suggests the contentment feeling of purring first—first get into the feeling of being at home, of trusting in the flow, the flow of the purring. The wink is the physical extension of the feeling and it links us in communion, in a sense of being together. There is no need for shyness. There is a natural flow of friendship and a natural exchange through the business at hand. We both feel at home and purrfect!

My Dream Titles Suggest Ideas about Using My Best Guess Solution

Meditations in Inspirational Writing: *Step 7*

Reread the description you wrote of your past peak experience and the personal motto you developed from that experience in Meditation Three, steps 8 and 9.

Close your eyes and imagine yourself going to visit a very wise person, a person who is the source of the wisdom expressed in your personal motto. Write an imaginary conversation with this person. Discuss your experiences working on your Dream Quest and your progress developing a solution to your problem. Get this wise person's comments on your progress and ideas for the future.

Hint: You might begin by discussing with this person your personal motto, because this person is the living example of the truth it expresses. That will help you bring this person's wisdom to life for you. Then proceed to discuss your efforts at problem solving.)

Example:
Me: (I approach a man who is performing some kind of dance-like exercise, perhaps something like tai chi. I see him moving his arms and legs smoothly in large, flowing patterns. He seems very peaceful, happy). Hello, there. May I talk with you?

Man: Well, hello there to you. Here, please join me for a moment. Just follow my motions.

Me: (I begin to make movements like his. I feel awkward at first, then I see him wink at me and I relax and find that my body is caught up in the movements quite automatically and effortlessly. It feels very good.)

Man: Well, now, you did very well. My name is Dr. Flow. How can I help you?

Me: I've been on a quest and I wanted to talk over my progress.

Dr. Flow: A quest? (I see him begin a little dance, mimicking someone searching.)

Me: Yes, I have been searching for a way to develop customers for my business and for a cure for my shyness.

Dr. F: My goodness! (I see him continue his little dance, expressing shyness, searching with scrutiny, exaggerated forehead wrinkle.) And how have you done? Has your quest been a success?

Me: (I see myself do a little dance for him, gesturing a welcome to him, inviting him into my space as I wink at him.) I have made progress, I think, for I have changed my focus, from worrying about myself and my thoughts about my inadequacies and what the person may be thinking about me to focusing on the other guy, taking time to extend a welcome of friendship and making the person feel at home.

Dr. F: Yes, I do like your little dance. (I see him begin to pick up on my dance and move into my space. We start dancing together. I follow his movements, then realize that he is following my movements. We simultaneously mirror one another and the source of our dance is beyond us—we are both being "danced" together. We start laughing.) I can see that it has helped you to overcome shyness. Has it helped you gain customers for your business?

Me: I think so, or it has made me less worried about it. I find that when I take the time to extend that at-home feeling, and we get to talking, it is fairly easy and seems to feel quite natural to learn about the person and find out how my business may be of use to the person. Sometimes my products and services themselves are of no use, but my approach, which is genuinely fun and relaxing for both of us, makes an impression.

Dr. F: That sounds excellent! (He does a little dance of exclamation and applause.) So what more do you need?

Me: Well, when it works, it works. But sometimes things seem a bit hectic, I may catch someone at a bad time, there may be a tension in the air, and I get thrown off a bit. (As I talk, I see Dr. Flow do another dance, mimicking someone acting in a very hectic manner, quite up-tight. He makes me laugh.)

Dr. F: Yeah, sometimes people don't want to relax and take it easy, even when it would really help them. Don't take it personally, just move along.

Me: That's good advice. Trying too hard isn't right—just move along.

Dr. F: Don't mind if I do. (He starts to dance away, making like a little gust of wind.) Remember the flow!

In Dialogue with a Very Wise Person, the Living Example of My Personal Motto, I Achieve a New Perspective on My Efforts at Dream Realization

....

....

....

....

....

....

....

....

....

....

....

....

....

....

....

....

....

In Dialogue with a Very Wise Person, the Living Example of My Personal Motto, I Achieve a New Perspective on My Efforts at Dream Realization

....

....

....

....

....

....

....

....

....

....

....

....

....

....

....

Meditations in Inspirational Writing: *Step 8*

Pick a dream (from the past week or earlier in your quest) that seems to most closely relate to your efforts to solve your problem. Use the ideas from the dream titles to guide your choice. As an alternative, pick a dream from anytime during this experiment that you feel is particularly related to your efforts in your Dream Quest.

Outline the action plot of this dream. Do a scenario analysis to find out what's happening in the dream. In extracting the action plot, replace particular nouns with indefinite pronouns (such as somebody, something), and emphasize the verbs in the dream—what is happening, the action. (See Meditation Two, Step 2).

Example:
Passing a friendly feeling, someone encounters something higher, communication exchange links them equally, and something continues.

The Action Plot of My Dream

....

....

....

....

....

....

....

....

....

....

....

....

....

....

....

....

....

Meditations in Inspirational Writing: *Step 9*

Write a sentence or two about how the action plot of this dream may reflect something about what you have learned during your Dream Quest. How has the development and improvement of your Best Guess solution, for example, taken you closer to the Focus of Your Quest? By what route of trial and error learning has your Best Guess improved? What have you learned? Let the action plot of the dream trigger answers to such questions.

Example:

I began with a Best Guess that was based on a trick, a diversionary tactic: beating shyness by thinking of the other guy and asking questions. But I was quickly brought back to the necessity of dealing with the feelings involved in the exchange. Passing by a friendly feeling reminds me how I can't pass this by, but must first tune into my image of comfortableness—being at home, having a friendly visit at home. Encountering something higher reminds me of how my focus gradually changed from worrying about my experience to being concerned with the other person's experience, a shift that changed the shyness quality surrounding meeting someone "in an elevated position" who could look down on me into a challenge, a challenge "higher" than overcoming shyness, a call to reach out and touch someone. Exchanging communication (in the wink) stresses the equality, the quality of "being in the same boat," which also served to change the situation to one less conducive to shyness. As the focus kept changing, apparently away from the issue of shyness and more into hospitality and good feelings, the feelings of shyness also seemed to disappear. Self-consciousness, at the root of shyness, seems to have been based on a feeling of alienation, of being separate from other things. Having the responsibility of hosting a friendly and comfortable meeting pulled me into the dance of life and shyness lost its roots.

The Action Plot of My Dream Reminds Me of What I Have Learned on My Dream Quest

....

....

....

....

....

....

....

....

....

....

....

....

....

....

....

....

....

Meditations in Inspirational Writing: *Step 10*

Rewrite your dream into as brief a form as possible. For example, can you condense your dream to only fifteen words? Pretend that you are sending a telegram of your dream. Pick fifteen words that are the most important and express most clearly the plot and significance of the dream.

Example:
Walking by friend's house, see cat in tree, wink each other, walk along.

I Rewrite My Dream Telegraph Style, Using a Few Important Words

Meditations in Inspirational Writing: *Step 11*

Pretend that each word represents a clue about your efforts at Dream Solutions, signifying something that you have learned about the solution of your problem. For each word in your shortened dream text, write out what that word suggests about your efforts in your Dream Quest.

Example:

Walking by: Don't be in a hurry. Take your time.

Friend: Be friendly. Extend friendship.

Cat: Cozy as a cat. Make people feel cozy.

Wink: Being joined in fun with the other person, no one to feel self-conscious.

Home: Feeling at home. Extend the at-home feeling to the other guy, help to feel at home with a friend.

The Words in My Condensed Dream Each Provide a Clue about My Efforts at "Dream Solutions"

Meditations in Inspirational Writing: *Step 12*

Gather your ideas about what you have learned in your Dream Quest from the three sources:

1. Your review of your past work and dreams (steps 1-6 above).

2. Your dialogue with your Wise Person (Step 7).

3. Your interpretive work with your chosen dream (steps 8-11).

Make some brief notes about what these sources indicate you have learned.

Example:
What I Have Learned from Review of Past Work:

Think of the other guy. Friendliness. Feeling at home. Wink in humor, touching, togetherness. Trust in the flow of the dance. Taking time out. Relate to customers as self, meeting their needs, helping them feel comfortable.

Dialogue with Wise Person:

Dr. Flow. Moving with the other person. A mirror, seeing ourselves reflected in the other person. When encountering resistance, move along, don't shove.

Dream Interpretation Work:

Don't pass up taking time out for the friendliness feeling. Purring, contentment, images of comfortableness. Reaching out. Don't assume the other person wants to remain aloof or distant. Hospitality.

Reviewing Past Work: I Note What I Have Learned

My Dialogue with a Wise Person: I Note What I Have Learned

The Interpretation of My Dream: I Note What I Have Learned

....

....

....

....

....

....

....

....

....

....

....

....

....

....

....

....

....

....

....

Meditations in Inspirational Writing: *Step 13*

As a final integrative act, write a poem about what you have learned from your Dream Solutions work. A good way to get started is to look through the material you wrote during this meditation and copy words and phrases that strike you as particularly meaningful or important. These could be:

Phrases from your descriptions of what you have learned

Words or phrases from your latest formulation of the Focus of your Quest or your latest Best Guess solution

Phrases used by your Wise Person

The title of your dream

Words or phrases from your evaluation of the action plot of your dream

Words or phrases from your dream itself

Words or phrases that you wrote based upon the word-clues in your dream

Other words or phrases that occur to you as you work on the poem

Example:
When shy, think of the other guy

Friendliness; make yourself at home; my friend's home

Trust in the flow of the dance

A wink in time saves worry; don't think — wink!

Take time to wink; out on a walk, taking time to enjoy life

Meeting, encounter: a dance, a chance

Winking together, being together in the dance

Contented cat at home in a tree; sly, shy cat

Words and Phrases from My Meditations: The Ones Most Meaningful or Significant

Meditations in Inspirational Writing: *Step 14*

Look over your list of words and phrases and see how you feel about them, what themes seem to emerge, what words or images repeat themselves. Then ask yourself, "What words and phrases in my list would I choose...

To describe my dream?"

To express my interpretation of this dream?"

To express what I have learned from Dream Solutions, or to describe what I now understand to be the solution to my problem, the answer to my question, or the fulfillment of the Focus of my Quest?"

For each of these categories, write the words and phrases you would use.

Example:
Dream: walk, friend's home, meet cat in tree, wink

Interpretation: encounter people, extend at-home feeling, wink, conspiratorial wink of togetherness, chance to dance, joining with other person

Realization: think of the other guy with a wink, extend a soft fuzzy, make the other person feel at home, doing business is feeling comfortable, what can I do for you

Words and Phrases to Describe My Dream

Words and Phrases to Describe My Interpretation of the Dream

....

....

....

....

....

....

....

....

....

....

....

....

....

....

....

....

....

....

Words and Phrases to Describe My Realization: What I Have Learned about the Answer to My Question

....

....

....

....

....

....

....

....

....

....

....

....

....

....

....

....

....

....

....

....

Meditations in Inspirational Writing: *Step 15*

Now try your hand at writing a free-form poem (rhyming doesn't matter) that accomplishes three things:

1. The poem tells the story of your chosen dream.

2. The poem expresses your interpretation of the dream.

3. The poem expresses some of your dream solutions, that is, what you have accomplished toward solving your problem, toward reaching the Focus of Your Quest.

To begin your poem, take those chosen words and phrases, change them around, and arrange them into a pleasing pattern, one that makes sense and feels right to you, one that tells your dream, gives your interpretation of the dream, and expresses what you have realized in your Dream Quest. Use as a title for your poem the same title you would use for the dream itself.

To write your poem, think of it as a brief arrangement of words that convey meaningful feelings, that capture or express some of the images you've encountered in your work on *Dream Solutions.* Don't be concerned about the format of the poem—rhyming and line length—but rather concentrate on finding words that match your feelings and imagery.

Example:
The Winking Cat
In walks of life I chance to meet
Strange things, new people, odd circumstances.
Shyness always beckons to me
I know it well, looking down on me
Like this cat up in a tree!
Yet it winks at me and I wink right back.
Winking together, being together!
What a dance is life!
There's always time to feel at home:
Here, let me show you how!

My Dream Realization Poem

Dream Solution: Haiku

Somewhat like a moment of self-realization, when you can look through the eyes of your dream's ultraconscious vision and experience some truth—that is dream solution. Creative writing—playing with the words in your dream record—often fosters dream solution. Sometimes it also provides an avenue of self-expression.

Dream solution and creativity require a relaxed, playful spirit. The limitations of a fixed form, however, may paradoxically stimulate such playful creativeness. Often, in fact, there can be no creativity without the presence of limits. If you are willing to accept and work with them, limitations breed transcendence. Here is a traditional poetic form whose limits provide an excellent opportunity for dream realization through creative writing—the Haiku.

Sev'nteen syllables
In lines of five, sev'n, five:
Image brings meaning.

Here's how to approach Haiku dream solution: Condense the essence of the dream into the first two lines. Use the third line to convey some truth about your life that correlates with the dream's vision.

Example:

Mouse flower blooming,
Unearth surprise, if you please.
Shyness winks at me.

While playing around with the words in your dream record and with new words that come to mind as you try to fit your writing into the form constraints of Haiku, you may discover new feelings about your dream images. In fact, Haiku is well suited to developing and expanding an impression of one dream image or symbol into a full expression of meaning.

Ugly face monster:
Hate, anger, rage—tears of rage!
Your eyes crave my love.

Haiku may also be effectively used to condense an entire dream into a concentrated, seventeen-syllable vision. The emotional impact of the dream is highly focused. The Haiku dream reveals the heart of the matter. It can be a superb method of dream expression. As a form of dream interpretation, Haiku dream solution can become an effective exercise in superimposing dream reality upon our ordinary vision.

Because the third Haiku line requires more patience and analysis than the other two, practice with the first two lines (Haiku dream symbol, Haiku dream). But if you can perceive in proper perspective the challenge of formal Haiku, a third line that presents an unexpected complement to the first two is both consistent with tradition and also yields valid dream solution.

Now you try it.

My Haiku Dream Solution

Dream Solution: Drawing

Make a drawing of your Dream Solution. Use symbols from your dream. You may also make a collage using pictures cut from magazines. You could use images that tell the story of your dream, suggest its interpretation, and show what you have learned, just as in your poem.

My Drawing of My Dream Solution

Pillow Letter: The Last Step

Carry your poem with you and read it every day for awhile to remind you of your inspiration and your success at dream solution. (Post your picture by your bed.) This, final, act of testimony will give you confidence in what success you did have, will encourage you to continue to apply your Best Guess solution for all it's worth, and will remind you that you can, when the itch returns, engage in a new cycle of creative problem solving, using this book or a method of your own invention.

Good Work!

This book has been through several revisions, incorporating the ideas of those who have used it in the past. The author welcomes your feedback, descriptions of what you gained from using it, and your comments. Send them to Henry Reed, 503 Lake Drive, Virginia Beach, VA 23451. *You'll receive a letter in reply.*

Appendix A:

A First-Person Account of Using "Dream Solutions"

There's No Need to Go Outside for Better Seeing
Margaret Dwyer

My first wholehearted attempt to "abide at the center of my being" was my experience using Henry Reed's *Dream Solutions*. It happened at a critical juncture in my life. I felt as though my back was against the wall, and both personal and professional doors were closing to me. I was anxious about my future and physically tired most of the time. I had decided I was going through a midlife change. Although I could intellectually understand this as "normal," even with its indescribable pain, that didn't stop me from being angry or confused about what to do.

I am now on the other side of that wall. I have gone through a transformation from who and what I thought I was to what I am truly becoming. My anger, confusion, and resistance have subsided. I am able to express myself in more creative ways. I am able to trust my inner voice and respond more appropriately. I have relaxed, let go, and become more agreeable to be with, both at home and at work. I have a sense of being on a fresh pathway, an adventure so searching and joyous that I can hardly remember my longing for public recognition, fame, and success. In short, I am discovering that there is far more to me than I had ever suspected.

In my teens and twenties, I believed I could have an important impact on the world and garner recognition in the molds of Madame Curie and Margaret Mead. Then, fifteen years in a difficult marriage forced me to reassess my purpose and goals and my beliefs about myself. Turning inward for guidance, I had a profound spiritual experience that revealed what I believe is my life's purpose. In the ten years since, I have struggled to make sense of that experience and to adjust to a difficult change in self-image from "world-renowned lecturer and author" to something much less attractive to me.

Without having resolved the self-image issue, I recently found myself, at forty-six, as an educator, administrator, and counselor, facing my own professional crisis in a deteriorating urban community college. I also saw myself as a wife in a second marriage, concerned about my husband's work, and a mother of three children, estranged for a year and a half from my twenty-two-year-old daughter.

Almost in desperation, I saw the Dream Quest as a new tool to work with. What follows is a personal report of that experience and its effect on my life.

Week 1: Focusing on the Quest

As I approached dreamwork for the first time, I was eager but apprehensive, determined to trust that dreams could produce the guidance I needed, yet terrified that they would! As instructed in the book, I collected my dreams for seven days and thought about several problems. For the first study night (on the seventh day), I had seven dreams to work with in my first Meditation in Inspirational Writing. The aim was to learn if my dreams guided me toward one problem for my focus during the dream quest.

Here's one dream:

I am in a senior citizen condominium trying to help out, going from one room to another in this vast complex. Several movie and music stars breeze in, captivate everyone, and breeze out. I feel left out, ineffective, wishing I could be accepted like the stars.

To capture the essence of the dream and simplify the process of comparing dreams, I titled each dream. This one was "Three's a Crowd: Helping Seniors and Stars." About this dream I wrote in my journal: "Sometimes I try to help out in situations even when my help is not wanted or appreciated. I wish I were a star instead of just helping others become stars themselves." My unfulfilled ambition to become a star in my profession is a sensitive subject to me.

Here's another dream:

I'm on a trip in the dark, an adventure. I'm excited and afraid. A voice says, "Don't be afraid; you've got your magic sword."

This reinforced another dream about being at a crossroads in my life. This one says I'm in the dark about my life, but I'm protected by what I interpret as the spiritual forces within me. When I started the book, I was concerned about my health, a career change, my daughter, my husband's work. The first week's dreams seemed to point to an underlying issue: My identity was tied to being wanted and helpful; how I felt about myself was related to being protected and loved. I was at a crossroads, wanted to take a turn for the better, but not knowing which way to turn. In my meditation journal, I wrote a dialogue between my questioning self and my knowing self:

"How will I ever be able to know what is the right thing to do?"

"You listen, and you understand, but you do not act, and not acting begins to dull your understanding."

I often avoided acting by being too "busy." Piling up on myself all the "helpful" things I had to do may actually have created more self-doubt and trouble, rather than less. From the quiet confidence radiated by my knowing self, I wrote: "I can be more truthful with myself and less demanding. I can take quiet action on the small things, a step at a time, and the larger problems will work themselves out."

As a result of this writing, I realized I no longer wanted to focus on "fixing" something in my external environment — my career or my relationship with my daughter. Instead, I wanted to focus on going deeper within myself and acting more confidently on what I found within. Waves of understanding washed over me, and I felt a sense of release.

My initial dream petition to be placed under my pillow each night simply said: "I'll listen to my inner voice first, then act. If I'm still feeling afraid or doubtful, then dreams, please show me a better way."

Week 2: Troubleshooting Mistaken Notions

I applied my affirmation conscientiously and collected a new set of dreams. I wrote in my journal: "I'm impressed that, as I listen to my inner voice and collect my dreams, I am having actual experiences in the day associated with my concerns."

Each time I came to a decision or a need for action, I quieted myself, listened to my inner voice, and acted accordingly. Tuning in to that voice demanded staying close to the center of my being, listening closely before any response. Instead of reacting to my world with fear and frustrated attempts to control others, instead of handicapping myself with anger and unhappiness, I found myself much calmer and quieter, more in control of myself. Frankly, sometimes it went well, sometimes not so well. But I concentrated on application.

I stopped trying to change the college, to get my daughter to communicate with me, to help my husband gain an important business contact. I also stopped rejecting what was happening to me, and two remarkable things happened.

First, I began to accept that my daughter was not contacting me, although that had been one of my deepest concerns. Then on the tenth day of the quest, she called to arrange a time to meet, as though we spoke to each other every day. I couldn't believe it. Nothing I had done in the last eighteen months had moved her to contact me. We met three days later, and, coincidentally, she wore a new hat of the same turquoise color as the suit I wore. The meeting went well; I concentrated on inner listening and guidance.

I also quit looking at how awful the college was becoming. I remained quiet as the organization continued to deteriorate. I also began to look for signs of new life, of transformation. How could I improve myself, my contribution to the college? Then, on the eleventh day, I met a man who changed my mind about looking for a position elsewhere. We began working together to further the research begun with my doctoral dissertation. We have since written a major grant to bring a large program for ethnic students into the college.

At the end of Week 2, following instructions, I reviewed my progress in fulfilling my application contract, seeking insights into how I may view my problem differently and compensate for anything I may have neglected or mistaken. Although I felt my initial efforts had gone well, I still had concerns about my health, about the stress at the college, and about my husband's work.

My study of one of the second week's dreams illustrates the value of this reappraisal and the recommended interpretation techniques:

A group of women is chatting around a round wooden table. Sunlight is streaming in through the windows. The walls of the room are painted yellow. Warmth and light surround the women. As I walk into the room they welcome me warmly and ask me to join them. I feel as though I have come home finally, am very feminine, and love it!

I interpreted this to mean that I had been welcomed by the feminine aspects of myself—those qualities of being warm, enlightened, yielding, intuitive, and accepting. As if I had "come home" to myself, I felt complete, aware, effective, in balance, and radiant. I realized that if I quit denying the feminine in myself—as I have been resisting the "woman's place is in the home" role—I would attain inner awareness and wholeness.

Dialoguing with a troubled image in another dream, I learned I was turning others off at work by being too forceful, demanding, and "masculine." In my career efforts, I had sacrificed many of my feminine aspects to the detriment of my inner life as well as my outer effectiveness. I would have to reduce the dominance of my male aspects and be more quiet and yielding to attune myself to the Higher Will. Thus I would feel "at home," accepted and loved, effective and once again powerful, but through enlightenment, not power games.

When I revised my Pillow Letter to strive for more feminine behavior, I did not remember dreams for a few days. I took that as a sign of resistance to my statement. So I revised it again to strive for more balance between the masculine and feminine aspects. I could bring the feminine into focus: being more receptive to others, more intuitive, more yielding, nurturing, and encouraging, yet without losing useful masculine traits: intellect, assertiveness, creativity, and strength of will.

Week 3: Searching with New Eyes

After this revision, my dream life flowed again. My inner voice became more real each day, and I felt more willing to listen to it and be guided by it. I liked myself better. I made a doctor's appointment, started an exercise class, bought some new clothes.

A dream from that week seemed reassuring:

I go to the doctor's for a checkup. The doctor is warm and funny. He looks like Mickey Rooney in a bright green Hawaiian shirt with yellow flowers on it. Through the walls of his inner voice, I can hear his staff discussing the progress of my life. He seems to feel I am healing. On the wall is a picture of the doctor looking like a guru with white robes. He is smiling, and out of the top of his head flows a rainbow down to a bright sun shining on his nose! Yellow light streams in through the window, and two men materialize to my amazement and hug me. A woman tries to materialize, but is only a shadowy figure, and then fades.

I woke up happy about this dream. The shadowy figure of a woman confirmed my need to strengthen the feminine, while hugs from the men released a fear that I was too masculine. "Going to the doctor" was indeed what I was doing, that is, seeking my inner voice and the healing forces within me. The humorous image of the doctor seemed to suggest that I should lighten up. The guru picture with the rainbow and the sunny nose seemed to say that I was "on the nose" with my spiritual quest.

In my journal, I reflected: "In trying to be more feminine, I find I have a lot of work to do on myself: weight loss, yielding, listening and responding more patiently to others. My resistance is very high. I heard a message today saying: You don't need sugar; you have me. Later in the day, however, someone brought me cookies and ice cream, and I ate them."

Part of my resistance to letting go and being more feminine is the fear that I will be left out or won't get to do some things in my life. This fear is ludicrous because my dreams say the male and female aspects have to be in balance, and one cannot dominate the other.

I'm still not sure about the best way to carry out my life purpose, such as being by my husband's side instead of in a career of my own. However, I'm going to act as though it's a fact and watch for signs of confirmation. As instructed by the book, I recalled a past experience when I said yes to a spiritual life of service, when I felt dedicated and at-one with life. I was utterly certain that a new age of consciousness was coming and that the part I was asked to play would be successful.

Through an exercise in which I rewrote the magic sword dream, I realized that, in spite of my spiritual commitment, I had been trying to go it alone, not sufficiently attuned on a day-to-day basis to the Higher Will. Perhaps I had intellectualized my commitment, and my dreams were returning me to the need for moment-by-moment contact with my inner voice if I am to fulfill my purpose. They suggest that, if I so listen and respond accordingly, I will be more effective professionally, more loving and understanding with my family, in better health with less stress, and more satisfied with and accepting of myself. My new revision of my Pillow Letter said:

"If I strive to become a clear, balanced channel of service to others not only by listening to my inner voice but also by responding fearlessly and in complete trust to its suggestions, yet still feel ineffective, then dreams, show me a better way."

Week 4: Taking Stock

The next dream was very moving for me:

A beautiful woman in riding clothes is training ponies. She befriends my young daughter and me. We move through her life, watching the men in her life fall in love with her while she is busy working. The dream shifts to an apartment where my daughter is playing with a mirror that cracks into fine pieces all over the carpet. My husband helps me pick up the pieces, but the feeling is that I didn't move fast enough to prevent the breakage or even to pick up the pieces myself, so he had to act. He's not happy to have to come to my rescue, but not condemning either. The dream fades back to the pony woman, still not certain who she chooses to love. Approaching her is a pony man who looks just like her. The feeling is that maybe this match will work.

To me, the pony woman symbolizes those aspects of myself that are developing my energies (ponies). Beautiful and competent, she focuses more on her work than on making a successful match with the male aspects (men in her life). The incident of the mirror seemed to say that my facades, my reflections, were cracking into many pieces. But because my daughter symbolizes new life and joy to me, the mirror breaking in her hands was a positive expression of the good that would result as my facade crumbled. That my husband was helpful but annoyed is very much the way he is. He loves me and respects my competence, but thinks I have often misdirected my energies instead of carefully listening to the Higher Will and responding. The pony man approaching at the end of the dream seems to verify that my efforts are working; listening to my inner voice, balancing the male and female aspects, then responding.

When I took this dream to a dream group for help, I began to cry, then shake. I couldn't stop letting go, in spite of the embarrassment and the pain of self-revelation to a group of strangers. Beyond the pain, this dream was telling me, "This time it will work out." Self-doubt, anger, confusion, and resistance were washing away. The worst was over; the storm had passed. This time I was coming together as a person. I felt my existence deeply and profoundly confirmed. No longer need I struggle to please others, realizing now how deeply and unconditionally we are loved as we are.

Two other dreams of the final week seemed significant. One suggested I should listen in a more concentrated way (meditation) to the rain (inner voice) tapping and often pounding on my roof (brain) and at my windows (soul).

Another dream suggested I don't listen enough. I felt these were telling me I should meditate more regularly, in addition to attending to my dreams.

The Dream Quest, in short, played a central role in my transformation. My dreams became a private haven from the storms of my personal and professional lives, storms I often created for myself. My dreams seemed not to blame, no matter what my struggle was. They guided me to hope and resolution. I saw my life reflected in them and, to my joy and amazement, the reflected image seemed more vivid than the one in my mirror.

The process was not an entirely gentle one. I had to review my personal commitment to an image I had held for many years. I had to reevaluate the shame and anguish, the bitterness and guilt I experienced over my divorce, my rebellion as a housewife, and the subsequent deaths of my parents. I was slammed in the face with my past in my daughter's rejection of me. And out of this, I have come to believe that the premise of this book is correct: Dreams will speak, sometimes dramatically, to those issues that occupy you during the day. They can become your inner companion with whom you can share your secrets and from whom you can expect support.

As for my daughter, our meetings have led us to new levels of mutual understanding. I came to realize the impact on a relationship when both individuals are going through a life-stage transformation. At twenty-two, she was experiencing an identity crisis not unlike mine at forty-six. In her anxiety about being ill-prepared to step out into the world alone as a professional dancer and teacher, she mirrored my dark side. She felt I was thoughtless, greedy, destructive, and blind to her needs. One of my dreams made clear the parallels of our individual struggles. Our different life-styles and goals had driven us apart, but this dream suggested that our love and respect were mutual, that is, if I accepted her world as being as significant to her as my world was to me.

Not every issue of concern in my life has been resolved, of course, but for the first time I am optimistic about what lies ahead, and I am more equipped than ever to go where adventure leads.

Appendix B:

A First-Person Account of Using "Dream Solutions"

A Dream Quest Experience
Joan Gravallese

The time was ripe, once again, to seek guidance from the invisible self—the self that is revealed when the conscious mind is laid aside in sleep. Sometimes it whispers to you, sometimes it leaps up and shouts, sometimes it must be almost forced into memory, sometimes its message is forgotten. Always, however, it is there, living a life that is woven inextricably with every waking hour.

Dreams have spoken to me before, during many sessions of dream groups and in a forceful experience of Jungian therapy. I was certain that I could now tap into that source of strength and depth and newness at this time when I felt blocked. When I ordered Henry Reed's *Dream Solutions*, the thought of four weeks of intensive dream work was in itself stimulating. What turned out to be the most revealing moments of that month's experiment I have chronicled here, as a tribute to the Life Force active in our dreams.

Week One: Getting Focused

The first week's written exercises (after collecting dreams for seven days) were concerned with the question of how to develop a focus for my quest and clarify my feelings with regard to it. Dream images showed a part of me that was starving, almost disappearing. Life seemed a treadmill of work, chores, and fatigue. I was ignoring those spheres of interest that motivated me greatly: religion, art, languages, music, the East. I felt too busy for those things and worked at my job and at home to exhaustion. I repeated to myself again and again, "No time, always rushing; where are my feelings?"

As I began the written analyses of the week's dreams, wonderful words sprang from my pen: "expression," "effusion," "brimming," "longing," "reaching," "changelessness," "giving." The feelings that these words conveyed were dimly starting to surface quite effortlessly and quite the opposite of the feelings occasioned by the situation troubling me. Instead of finding time and effort to do all my longed-for activities, my dreamwork suggested that I should simply allow a little mental time and those activities would be done in me. I must not revive my interests; they would revive me. What a surprise!

And then, another surprise. One of the guided exercises encouraged me to contact inner guidance by simply having an imaginary dialogue between the me who is troubled and the me who can solve problems. Startling thoughts emerged when I presented my problem:

"How can I be a good nurse and serve others and at the same time be relaxed, rested, in touch with my husband, have time for meditation, prayer, and all the other things I like to do?"

I was told to follow my heart, to do at every moment what fills my heart. Only then would I enjoy the moment and not rush.

The inner guidance spoke on:

"Do what is most important and leave the details undone if need be. Pray to God for peace and calmness between every two things you do. This will not give you time for what you need; this is part of what you need. Cut out anything that separates you from the Spirit—job included."

So the initial formulation of my quest materialized and I was able to put it into words: "How can I change my attitude and my situation to serve others in nursing, be there for my husband, be relaxed, and have time for people and other interests?"

It appeared that the problem was caused only partly by the situation; the rest was caused by my attitude. Without changing that, even a nine-day week would not satisfy my racing agenda. The question of perspective became clear. In the long run, the essence remains, but details of work fade away. As Emerson said, "Spare moments are like uncut diamonds to be fashioned for lasting beauty."

In response to the book's instructions to devise a tentative plan of action, a contract with myself, I therefore decided on several concrete things to do to achieve my quest, and I asked my dreams every night of the second dream week to show me a better way if this tentative approach failed.

Week Two: Befriending Troubles

The next seven nights brought an abundance of dreams and daily effort to change my behavior. I slept a little more, spent some time on art, music, languages, and nutrition. I also meditated a little longer and took a few moments to pray for calmness between the things I did. I felt a little more relaxed, though still tired, and more satisfied to have spent time on the spiritual and the artistic. On the days I prayed for calmness, I was more conscious of the actual things I was doing instead of the number of things to do. One unexpected discovery was that I found myself more personable, interacting more with people and expressing myself more.

Performing the written exercises at the conclusion of the second week revealed how my dreams very clearly portrayed problems in my attitudes. In one dream I visit my parents' house and see how I learned from them to work compulsively. The tendency to a stubborn desire for perfection and simply overdoing it appeared and was strongly criticized by a dream character who was easy-going and did not take everything so seriously. In another dream my husband and I missed a bus because of my rushed agenda. We had been headed for Cape May, a favorite vacation spot filled with nature, beauty, and peace. And still another dream showed that when I left my place of work, I saw, beautifully arranged on the sidewalk, antiques, artwork of lovely colors and European influence, and artifacts from the sea. A somewhat amusing symbol pursued me in another sequence: a female derelict from Virginia Beach who was pleasant, educated, and likable, but very much in need of care.

By turning these symbols round and round, I discovered that I was missing the essence of what I needed by concentrating on details, though the details were worthwhile. Because of my desire to squeeze in every activity even at the last minute, I lost sight of the Spirit within, Who could lead me to the answer I needed and Who is peace, beauty, art, and nature. The dreams were saying that my husband and I must wait for the Spirit, our "bus," our vehicle to take us to the perfect place of peace. Wait—not work, not rush.

How well this advice responded to my dream quest! My efforts to change my behavior during the week also related to the dream content. Concentrating on the inner life of dreams, sleeping more, reading, meditation, involvement with art, music, languages, and study—all these actions led to a little less hurrying and more reliance on feelings. There seemed to be the beginning of making room for the spiritual and intuitive sides of me and rest for the physical body.

One writing exercise involved a dialogue with a "troublesome image." I chose to interact with the symbol of the derelict. She had a great deal of interesting things to tell. She also insisted upon being cared for! We came to a bargain: I would let her rest, feed her, and fix her up, and she would accept this treatment and teach me all she knew about entering into myself and slowing down. She would remind me of the values I encountered in my involvements with A.R.E. (Association for Research and Enlightenment) at Virginia Beach.

The blocked feeling I had when I began using the book did not seem pertinent any longer. I realized, however, that change is not easy, and touching emotions is sometimes difficult for me. The part of me that is mechanical and compulsive tends to be defensive when criticized. Letting go of this did not seem like a big sacrifice at this point when compared to the benefits that spring from growth in the directions I favored. The key words became "balance" and "perspective."

The conclusion of this week's writing exercises involved a revision of my goals of action for the next week. For my daily contract I decided to follow these principles: Think of the correct perspective before doing anything. Pray between all things. Consider a four-day work week. Each day read something satisfying about the spiritual life (Monday), the psychic (Tuesday), nutritional therapies (Wednesday), travel (Thursday), dreams (Friday and Saturday). Sleep more, and above all, meditate with full attention.

I prepared my petition (a Pillow Letter to my dreams that I would sleep on) for the third dream week: I will try to be rested, peaceful, in touch with God, art, and beauty, and I will try not to be compulsive, so that the richness that is inside may fill me and heal the neglected person within. If I can't keep my actions and feelings in the right perspective, then, dreams, show me a better way.

Week Three: A Creative Encounter

The third week was pivotal. New dream symbols were brought forth and the struggle to change behavior continued. I was not too successful in sleeping more or in achieving peace, but I was acutely aware of the part of me that tried to forbid these new things. Also, I noticed that the dreams did not focus on practical things as I had done before starting this experiment—such as how to save time at work or in household activities. The change of attitude was emphasized in the dreams, which seemed more than ever to be the key to a solution.

This week's dream symbols were exciting: visiting relatives, teacups, horses, Oriental dance, growth, plants and replanting, exotic Egyptian eyes, more dance, a lovely old house, a jailbreak in Madrid. But again there appeared a symbol of the neglected person: a young woman, looking sick and undernourished, with her hair cut off. Uncertainty about a new approach was shown by another young woman about to do an Oriental dance on ice skates accompanied by another woman. She needed little practice, but her outfit was wrong for the part and she also had to spend some time waking up her dance partner for the rehearsal.

An important writing exercise of this week was to converse with a novel dream symbol to find out its role and special qualities and to see what light it might shed on the Dream Quest. The most intriguing symbol in the week's dreams was a reddish brown horse being led down the staircase of a guest house in Cape May (the spot my husband and I could not reach because we missed the bus in the previous week's dream). Two teenage girls took the horse through the living room into a backyard filled with yellow flowers. My husband and I were looking for a place to stay and decided that this strange house was not it.

I therefore found myself in the unusual position of speaking to the horse. The result was one of the best conversations I've had with a symbol. What was the horse doing in a run-down guest house? Trying to get out, of course. The backyard would make it much happier. The horse was filled with energy and needed too much exercise to be confined. It needed to run for pure enjoyment; it wanted to feel the sun and see green grass and flowers. This horse reminded me that it was the same earthy color as one I colored as a child, one that was criticized by my mother. It then asked me if I wanted to go for a ride! The time had to be right for it to be led outside, it said. Now that it was out of the house, my husband and I could go in and fix it up.

The horse said that we'd be very happy because something that was confined no longer is. I asked the horse if it was my creative side. "Only the energy behind your creative side. You colored me, remember?" The horse said that it was helping me to be peaceful and in touch with what I love. "When energy is let out as it should be, there is enough to fill you so you can get your house in order. If you leave the house, you've missed the boat. If you try to fix the house with me inside, I'll undo it. But, with me out, you're free." The horse also told me to let chores wait, feel happy to be alive, and to do what satisfies my soul first. "Use energy on the right things and it will multiply." It advised me to pray first, feel the sun, sit down and draw, and spend more affection on my husband.

Another writing exercise had me describe a peak experience from the past and write a motto for it. I remembered an afternoon several years ago when I was home drawing and suddenly felt exhausted, lifted to a plane of feeling where I was part of all created things—part of nature, part of the force of life. My essence and the essence of nature seemed the same. I was compelled to draw what I felt, and the result was a vibrant young woman in a dress made of leaves, climbing a giant vine of large tropical leaves. Two mottoes came to mind to describe the truth that was expressed in that experience: "In You we live and move and have our being" and "Life is one."

As instructed by the book, I rewrote the horse dream with my peak experience and mottoes in mind to see how I might have acted differently. In the new version, my husband and I saw the horse and followed it out to the backyard. We petted it and enjoyed the sun and the grass. We felt part of the nature in that lovely place. The two girls smiled at us and silently left. Renewed with energy, we went back into the house and thought about buying it, fixing it, and opening a guest house. In other words, we followed our instinct instead of rejecting it. This suggested to me that before plunging into work, we must first renew ourselves by becoming one with the Life Force. In practical terms, follow our instincts, sleep more, meditate in the morning, take the sun, and be out in nature more on the weekends. Let the spirit run free, which would give us all the energy we needed for the week.

These insights fit in with my Dream Quest, and new ideas emerged. I was still focusing too much on things, even though they were the things that would satisfy my soul. Instead, I felt that I must follow the Life Force and incorporate it into all I do. How could that be done? The answer suggested itself: Follow any impulse, however slight, that draws me to God, peace, nature, beauty. This meant looking at trees and flowers on the way to work, gazing at the sky, eating lunch in the park and not inside, sleeping more to replenish the Force, looking for the life in every person I met and praying for them, eliminating rushing, meditating, reading, and asking for a four-day work week. These things would constitute the contract with myself for the next week.

My Dream Quest was slightly modified with all this in mind: I will seek the Life Force, let it draw me to it so that I may be rested and peaceful; in touch with God, my husband, art, and beauty; and I will let go of compulsiveness, let it melt in the Life Force, so that the richness that is inside may be nourished by that Force, so that it may heal the neglected person within. If I can't keep my actions and feelings in the right perspective so that this will happen, then, dreams, show me a better way.

Week Four: Inspiration Realized

Thus I approached the last week of the Dream Quest experiment. Every day I tried to keep the contract. Some moments I was very successful and enjoyed the time immensely. I felt closer to God, meditated more, followed impulses more, and showed more feelings with others. At other times, the compulsiveness won. But I felt that I had a handle on the new approach of seeking union with the Life Force. One important outcome was that I finally decided to work only four days a week. This was approved by my head nurse and I felt elated.

Tentatively, the solution to my problem seemed to be not merely more time, but also seeking the Kingdom of God first, contacting nature next, and trying to put all things in the right perspective. Contacting the Life Force first would make energy multiply. It would loosen the life within me so that I may use it for people and for the right things in the right way. Its abundance would spill over into all activities.

My dream experiment had so far brought me closer to my real feelings. I learned that I could contact people better and follow my impulses better when other parts of me were satisfied. I realized again that I must follow the slightest impulse to the infinite.

Among the dreams of the final week was one with my husband and me moving into a new apartment. It was large, elegant, religious, filled with art and Middle Eastern objects, and had just been vacated by a psychic friend of ours. It was also near my job and would save commuting time. This new dwelling meant room for expansion.

In another dream, the apartment was being shown to us by a woman I know, who took the role of real estate agent. In reality this person was always tired because she was starved for beauty and art and tried to satisfy all her artistic needs by working eighteen hours a day; in the dream she looked rested, lovely, with a new outfit and hair style. This hopeful symbol was quite a change from the derelict lady of a couple of weeks ago—a true "agent" of change! The only flaws in the apartment were the frenetic shocking pink walls (showing that my compulsion was still alive), a clogged drain, and rich wooden floors covered over with old beige carpeting. There was work to be done, but the price for all this was less than my present rent. So it appeared that I would be working at healing myself for less output of time and money and energy. Another dream showed repairs being made on the walls.

The last dream of the week was a war scene in which I was being attacked by an army of soldiers in my parents' house. I plotted various ways of destroying their power before it destroyed me. I survived and felt the dread of going into the house to clear out the corpses.

These dreams showed a change: a new dwelling, representing myself and the house of my spirit; a battle that was won, representing the beginning of a change of attitude.

An important writing exercise in this final week's dreamwork was to let a dialogue emerge between myself and the Wise Person that had given me the dreams, the dream mottoes, and the peak experience of several years ago. My mind was pulled to a figure I had discovered several years ago, conversed with then, and even painted. To my surprise, the image was as real to me now as then. She was still sitting in her forest, surrounded by leaves, gazing at a lake as still as a mirror; still there in her flowing robes, lovely as a Grecian goddess, all serenity and peace. Her advice to me glowed, and still does:

"I am always here, within you. Do you see me rushing, cramming, compulsive? Yet, I have peace at my feet. I do not study, but I have the wisdom of the ages. My link is with the Life Force, the Spirit, the spark of God within. It gives me sustenance, all that I need. It is reflected in my lake. You have only to call me, come sit at my side, gaze at the deep waters, and you, too, will find peace. Think of me when you are harried. I am in you, unhurried. I will be your anchor. I will lead you to the Infinite you yearn for, through stillness, quiet, nature. You must have your link to nature. Do not forget it. The sun, sky, wind, rain, trees, plants—all these will give you life. During the day, wear your white (uniform). It is the symbol of purity and service. Give the Life Force to others during the day. But take off the white at night and don yourself in all the colors of the palette. Paint all the colors. Paint your plants and vines, and bless all that is living around you. You are God's instrument. Let His Spirit guide you as the water in my lake guides the leaves that fall upon it. Take my hand when you are tired or frightened or harried. For Life is always within you. And peace is at your doorstep. The world may howl about you, but you are safe in my forest."

The impact of these words was tremendous. They flowed from some inside source and reduced me to tears. How could such an answer be given to a problem I posed four weeks ago? And how could it come from within, when for months I had kept trying to change things without? We must always look in amazement and humility at the resources we have, given to us by the Spirit.

To end the project, the book instructed me to write a poem about a dream, its interpretation, and the realizations derived from the Dream Quest, a long poem developed about the entire experience. The instructions also explained how to write a briefer version, a three-line Haiku. This short poem rushed out instantly, ready-made:

> *Life Force exploding,*
> *Channel unblocked and flowing.*
> *Peace is within me.*

The effect of what I learned stayed with me for many weeks. I felt revitalized. I tried to fix up my "new dwelling" and respond to the feelings that arose, though the battle with over-extending was far from over. For several months I dreamt of guest houses, Cape May, and the peace it symbolized. One added and very unexpected benefit from the entire experience was that I was drawn inward by a great desire to meditate, as though some invisible fisherman were reeling me in with no effort on my part. This feeling insists upon being obeyed while it is with you, or else it fades as imperceptibly as it comes.

A chronicle of this dream experiment can never be as deeply vital as the experience itself, but the truth expressed still touches me and still has the power to renew and refresh me. From time to time I read what I wrote in *Dream Solutions* and meditate on my poem. I am grateful for having had the opportunity to touch once again that deeper part of me—the Life Force.